Two Careers/ One Family

The Promise of Gender Equality

Lucia Albino Gilbert

Sage Series on Close Relationships

 SAGE Publications
International Educational and Professional Publisher
Newbury Park   London   New Delhi

Copyright © 1993 by Sage Publications, Inc.

For information address:

SAGE Publications, Inc.
2455 Teller Road
Newbury Park, California 91320

SAGE Publications Ltd.
6 Bonhill Street
London EC2A 4PU
United Kingdom

SAGE Publications India Pvt. Ltd.
M-32 Market
Greater Kailash I
New Delhi 110 048 India

Printed in the United States of America

Library of Congress Cataloging-in-Publication Data

Gilbert, Lucia Albino
Two careers/one family / Lucia Albino Gilbert.
        p. cm. —(Sage series on close relationships)
    Includes bibliographical references and index.
    ISBN 0-8039-5072-1 (cl). —ISBN 0-8039-5073-X (pb).
    1. Dual-career families—United States. 2. Sex role—United
States. I. Title II. Title: 2 careers, one family. III. Series.
HQ536.G534   1993
306.872—dc20   92-42026

93 94 95 96   10 9   8   7   6   5   4   3   2

Sage Production Editor: Diane S. Foster

£12·50

Two Careers/
One Family

SAGE SERIES ON CLOSE RELATIONSHIPS

Series Editors
Clyde Hendrick, Ph.D., and
Susan S. Hendrick, Ph.D.

In this series...

Contents

To the two loves of my life, my husband, Jack, and my daughter, Melissa, and to my parents, Carmelina and William

Series Editors' Introduction

When we began our work on love attitudes more than a decade ago, we did not know what to call our research area. In some ways it represented an extension of earlier work in interpersonal attraction. Most of our scholarly models were psychologists (though sociologists long had been deeply involved in the areas of courtship and marriage), yet we sometimes felt as if our work had no professional "home." That has all changed. Our research not only has a home, but it has an extended family as well, and the family is composed of relationship researchers. Over the past decade the discipline of close relationships (also called personal relationships and intimate relationships) has emerged, developed, and flourished.

Two aspects of close relationships research should be noted. The first is its rapid growth, which has resulted in numerous books, journals, handbooks, book series, and professional organizations. As fast as the field grows, however, the demand for even more research and knowledge seems to be ever increasing. Questions about close, personal relationships still far exceed answers. The second noteworthy aspect of the new discipline of close relationships is its interdisciplinary nature. The field owes its vitality to scholars from communications, family studies and human development, psychology (clinical, counseling, developmental, and social), and sociology as well as other disciplines such as nursing and social work. It is this interdisciplinary wellspring that gives close relationships research its diversity and richness, qualities that we hope to achieve in the current series.

The **Sage Series on Close Relationships** is designed to acquaint diverse readers with the most up-to-date information about various topics in close relationships theory and research. Each volume in the series covers a particular topic or theme in one area of close relationships. Each book reviews the particular topic area, describes contemporary research in the area (including the authors' own work, where appropriate), and offers suggestions for interesting research questions or real-world applications related to the topic. The volumes are designed to be appropriate for students and professionals in communication, family studies, psychology, sociology, and social work, among others. A basic assumption of the series is that the broad panorama of close relationships can best be portrayed by authors from multiple disciplines so that the series cannot be "captured" by any single disciplinary bias.

The current volume, *Two Careers/One Family*, takes us to the frontier of close relationships, where traditional gender roles are being reevaluated in light of what is both functional and optimal for persons in dual-career partnerships. Unlike most other books in the series, the current volume cannot summarize the past—for dual-career relationships, there is virtually no past. Thus the book describes the current world of women and men trying to negotiate new realities at home and at work, with each other and with the larger social structure. It also offers a glimpse of the future and the potential that exists for creative restructuring of our concepts of gender.

CLYDE HENDRICK
SUSAN S. HENDRICK
SERIES EDITORS

Preface

In many ways the feminist movements of the 20th century pro-vided a powerful challenge to traditional patterns of marriage. Yet, they strengthened marriage as an institution by giving women and men greater freedom to enter into a relationship in which the needs for interconnection and separateness can be expressed and accepted by both partners. The emergence and rapid growth of two-career families reflect in part the positive effects of feminism on hetero-sexual relationships. Though my book describes many of the diffi-cult aspects of this emerging family form, I hope ultimately this work will stand as a celebration of love and intimacy between partners who believe gender equality is desirable and possible.

Interestingly, discussions of dual-wage heterosexual families often overlook the uniqueness of the dual-career family and how, in theory, it challenges traditional notions of gender. Women employed in low-paying jobs is neither a new nor a radical concept and thus does not necessarily challenge traditional assumptions about a woman's place. In contrast, the concept of women and men as equally able economic providers presents a dramatically different view of how to accomplish work and family goals. It is a view that assumes certain changes in women's and men's self-concepts as well as in societal norms and structures. Also overlooked are the facts that not all dual-career families are heterosexual and that the integrating and sharing of occupational and family roles, which is "emerging" for women and men in heterosexual dual-career relations, is normative among lesbians and gay men.

This book has three main sections. Because social environments are crucial to understanding personal relationships and individual behavior, the three chapters in Part One describe the societal context of young adults today. The three chapters in Part Two then address in some detail both the expectations for and realities of dual-career family life. Part Three, "What's Ahead," looks to the future. Only selected references on dual-career families and gender are included for practical purposes. Also, I well know that the organizational and social views of women and men, and the constraints and opportunities they envision, vary by race and ethnicity as well as by sexual orientation. Many of my conclusions are based on studies that did not necessarily include diverse populations or compare individuals by ethnicity, race, or sexual orientation when diverse populations were included in a study. Also, given my interest in gender equality, my comments most directly apply to relationships among members of heterosexual, dual-career families. Finally, the literature, and hence this book, uses the terms *two-career family* and *dual-career family* interchangeably.

In Chapter 1, "Societal Changes and Realities: An Introduction to the Dual-Career Family," I use current educational and employment statistics to frame the social reality for today's young adults. I then discuss the enormous changes these data imply in conceptions of gender and of roles traditionally assigned to members of one sex or the other. Emerging views of how gender processes tied to biological sex operate in our society also are described. Particularly important to the purposes and goals of the book is explicating how many of the constraints implicit in the heterosexual two-career family form are inextricably tied to gender processes.

Chapters 2 and 3, "Contemporary Female Perspectives" and "Contemporary Male Perspectives," respectively, detail ways in which social learning, interpersonal ways of behaving, and social practices and institutions influence women's and men's self-concepts and choices about occupations and family life. Key concepts include the notions of female and male dependency, the prerogative of male superiority, and the meaning of personal achievement.

Part Two focuses on living as a two-career family and patterns of combining family and occupational work. Chapter 4, "Young Adults' Career and Family Intentions and Expectations," describes findings from my own extensive research on college women's and men's intentions and expectations for career development, marriage, and marital partners. Chapter 5, "Living as a Dual-Career Family," summarizes the large, complex literature that exists on couples who have entered into this kind of intimate relationship. Any discussion of work and family must eventually turn to the structure of occupations and the benefits provided to employees. The personal lives of individuals unfold within the constraints of societal norms, values, and institutions. Thus, Chapter 6, "Workplace Family Policies," describes changes in workplace policies and what we know about the effects of these changes on employee well-being and corporate profit.

Part Three then addresses the future. In Chapter 7, "What Will the Future Bring for Gender Equality and Dual-Career Families?" I anticipate what is ahead for young adults who will be partners in two-career families. I make predictions about the benefits of increased gender equity for same-sex and heterosexual dual-career couples and identify continuing obstacles and sources of stress for partners in dual-career families in general.

Overall I remain very positive about the future of dual-career families and see the focus on gender processes as enlightening and instructive. I especially ask readers to keep an open mind. Basically this book is about dramatic social change, and change never comes easily—even for those women and men who want it.

Collecting the material for and writing this book has been very rewarding personally. Genuine gratitude goes to the many friends, colleagues, students, clients, and participants in research studies who shared their thoughts and experiences with me and, by so doing, helped me to understand the importance of gender in our day-to-day lives. Discussions with Connie Deutsch, Natalie Eldridge, Ted Huston, Sherwin Davidson, Michael Toth, and Joe Ann Watson always left me thinking as did meetings with the members of my research team, Karen Rossman, Marybeth Hallett, Brian Thorn, and Karen Habib. Mary Dewar, a special friend who now lives many miles away, sent me wonderful articles and references she correctly surmised would not have come to my attention otherwise. Lydian Reed is warmly thanked for her assistance with typing references and attending to the many details of style and format.

I am especially appreciative of Murray Scher, Connie Deutsch, Karen Rossman, Jack Gilbert, and Melissa Gilbert, all of whom so conscientiously read and reread parts or all of the manuscript and offered excellent, thoughtful comments. Karen Rossman made numerous trips to the library on my behalf, provided me with any pertinent material that crossed her path, and eagerly participated in many dialogues on gender. Connie Deutsch was a constant source of inspiration and good sense and never tired of my needing to talk something over. Murray Scher's eye for clarity and precise writing was enormously helpful. My husband Jack's ability to critique material outside his own area of scholarship (chemistry) continues to amaze me. His interest in my work and in our life together goes far beyond the ordinary. Melissa, our daughter, checked all the references and quotations used in the book and worked with me on the book's revisions and index. In many ways the motivation and energy to take on this project came from her. She is such a wonderful young woman, and, in writing this book, I wanted to do whatever more I could to help make the world a better place for her and her friends.

This work would not have been possible without support from the University of Texas Research Institute. Grants from the Research Institute funded studies reported in the book and a Faculty Research Leave awarded to me by the institute allowed me the time to complete the book.

Susan and Clyde Hendrick also made this book possible. I was delighted when they asked me to do a book for the new **Sage Series on Close Relationships** and could not be more pleased with their wisdom and guidance as editors. Very special appreciation goes to Ann McMartin for her marvelous illustrations, and very special thanks are due Terry Hendrix at Sage Publications for putting me in touch with Ann as well as for making the illustrations possible.

Finally, I want to acknowledge my parents, Carmelina and William Albino, both now 80 years of age and in good health. Their visions for their children were instrumental to our life paths. My brother and I both live in dual-career families.

LUCIA ALBINO GILBERT

ONE

The Societal Context of Young Adults Today

1

❦

Societal Changes and Realities: An Introduction to the Dual-Career Family

Fate, Time, Occasion, Chance, and Change? To these All things are subject but Eternal Love. (Shelley, 1829/1965, p. 107)

One of my favorite indicators of social change is *The Wall Street Journal,* a highly conservative newspaper concerned primarily with money, power, and corporate culture. Bylines from current issues tell us "Men Become Evasive About Family Demands" (because of fear of being honest with male bosses who just would not understand), "Bright, Young Women Bring Home the Bacon" (today's young women, aged 25 to 29, are just as likely to have four or more years of college as young men and are just as likely to be employed), "Wedding Bells Ringing Later—But More Often" (young adults are not marrying as soon as they used to, but more people are giving marriage a try during their lives; the median age at first marriage today is 23.6 years for women and 25.9 years for men), "More Job Seekers Put Family Needs First" (and look for companies that recognize family responsibilities), and "Young Women Insist on Career Equality, Forcing the Men in Their Lives to Adjust" (young career women aren't playing follow the leader any more, and that's causing problems with the men in their lives).

As these bylines suggest, "fate, time, occasion, chance, and change" are dramatically altering views of work, family, and intimate relationships, but not our willingness to seek eternal love. Certain social changes brought about the possibility of dual-career families; the increasing numbers of such families are bringing about still other changes. This chapter explains why the dual-career family represents social change and theoretically moves us beyond conventional forms of work and intimate relationships. I first describe what is meant by the term *dual-career family* and then examine certain core assumptions crucial to its representing gender equality. I then present in some detail recent theoretical perspectives on gender that provide a heuristic framework for understanding the experiences of women and men in the 1990s, especially those entering dual-career relationships.

❧ The Dual-Career Family as an Indicator of Social Change

In 1969, the Rapoports, working in England, first used the term *dual-career family* to describe what they considered to be an unusual and "revolutionary" type of dual-wage heterosexual family that emerged as the result of complex social changes. Revolutionary from their perspective was the dual-career families' apparent inconsistency with respect to traditional notions of gender. In these families, the woman and the man both pursued a lifelong career, relatively uninterrupted, and also established and developed a family life that often included children. Contrary to tradition, women in these families viewed their employment as salient to their self-concept and life goals and pursued occupational work regardless of their family situation. Male partners, in turn, appeared less defined by the traditional "good provider role" long associated with male privilege and power (Bernard, 1981).

The notion of a two-career family was met with both excitement and skepticism. It promised to preserve the best of marriage—intimacy and enduring love—but freed partners from the harness of gender roles. True equality between women and men—social, economic, and political equality—seemed highly possible, if not inevitable. Now, some 20 years later, both the excitement and the skepticism appear realistic. Although increasing numbers of couples establish dual-career relationships, the larger promise of true equality has yet to be achieved. The reasons for this become clear when we look more closely at assumptions implicit in viewing the dual-career family as an egalitarian family form and what these assumptions require in the way of social change. Before we look at the assumptions it is helpful to first review current facts on working women and men in the United States. These facts and figures describe the broader social context of dual-career families today.

Facts and Figures

Women today have more opportunities for education and career placement and advancement than ever before in our history. In 1970 only one quarter of women aged 25 to 34 had any college experience, compared with 35% of men the same age. By 1985, 45% of women and 48% of men aged 25 to 34 had completed at least one year of college, with 22.5% of women and 25% of men having completed four or more years of college education (U.S. Department of Education, 1988). Currently young women and men (aged 25 to 29) are equally likely to have four or more years of college. Women also experience fewer barriers to using their education, and a sizable number have entered professional fields formerly closed to them, such as medicine, law, and university teaching. In 1990, women represented 25% of full-time employed physicians, 27% of lawyers, 30% of college and university teachers, and 36% of Ph.D. psychologists (National Science Foundation, 1991; U.S. Department of Labor, Women's Bureau, 1991). Moreover, women now constitute about 39% of the professional labor force, compared with only 26% in 1960. The percentage of women is higher among students currently enrolled in business, law, or medical schools and other kinds of graduate programs. In 1991, for example, women accounted for 33% of law students, 37% of medical students, and 51% of doctoral psychology students.

A direct corollary of women's increased educational and occupational opportunities is the dramatic increase in the number of U.S. families in which both partners report full-time employment. Work is an important component of contemporary women's and men's identity and well-being (Betz & Fitzgerald, 1987). Current norms assume not only that single and married men will work but also that single and married women will work. Today, only 10% of U.S. families fit the traditional model of a two-parent family with children, a wage-earning husband, and a homemaker wife. Even among two-parent heterosexual families, the proportion where the husband is the only wage-earner has dropped to 20%; for minority families it is even lower (Spain, 1988). For married women with children under 6 years old, 59.2% are in the labor force, and of these, 69.6% are employed full-time. For married women with children under the age of 18, these percentages increase to 67% employed and 72.9% of these employed full-time. The average working wife with full-time employment contributes approximately 40% of the family's annual income (U.S. Bureau of Labor Statistics, 1991).

The fact that more women view occupational work in professional fields as central to their self-identity obviously increases the number of families with partners who both consider themselves in careers (as opposed to women moving in and out of the work force depending on family needs). As Chapter 2 explains, heterosexual women, more than heterosexual men, assume and push for the "revolutionary" two-career family envisioned by the Rapoports (Ferree, 1990; Gilbert, 1988; Guelzow, Bird, & Koball, 1991). Although women on average still do more of the family work, men increasingly are involving themselves in home roles and parenting (Barnett & Baruch, 1987b; Pleck, 1985, 1987). If we look at only dual-career families, research indicates that approximately one third of heterosexual and most lesbian and gay partners do establish what they and objective others would consider an egalitarian relationship (Eldridge & Gilbert, 1990; Gilbert, 1985; Hodnett, 1991).

Overall, then, we see an increase in the number of families in which both spouses pursue careers and establish a family life together—the family form identified by the Rapoports in 1969. We also see women and men both looking to family and occupational work as sources of well-being and fulfillment. To what degree do these findings represent social change with regard to the promise of gender equality?

The Closing Gender Gap

I now turn to the assumptions mentioned earlier, assumptions implicit in viewing dual-career families as egalitarian. There are three:

Assumption 1. Equality exists between the partners economically, which in turn implies for heterosexual couples an economic equality between women and men.

Assumption 2. There is a compatibility of occupational and family systems, that is, of work and family.

Assumption 3. Partners' self-concepts allow for the establishment of a relationship characterized by role-sharing and mutuality and by an interdependency free of the constraints of gender. Particularly crucial to the relationships between women and men are the related assumptions that neither partner would expect women to accommodate to an assumed male superiority or expect men to have authority over women.

Assumption 1 makes clear the dramatic and revolutionary nature of the dual-career family form. The sexes never have been equal economically. A crucial part of patriarchy was men's unquestioned greater economic power and entitled access to resources. The importance of this first assumption in achieving gender equality cannot be overemphasized. Historically women depended on men economically and were not taken seriously as providers, even in those instances when they were able to achieve the necessary education and credentials. Women were not supposed to have "independent means" because men were their eventual and natural benefactors.

Where do women and men stand on this today? Women have made some progress since 1969, when their median annual earnings were 59% of what men earned. By 1985 that ratio had risen to 63.3 cents per dollar earned by men and, by 1990, to 71 cents. Regardless of how one measures wages and adjusts for relevant factors, the same substantial earnings gap results (Horrigan & Markey, 1990). In nearly every occupational area, men earn more than women. Representative figures for full-time employed women's earnings as a percent of men's earnings in 1990 were 70.4% for lawyers, 76.1% for social scientists, and 82.0% for physicians. Still, today the median annual income of female college graduates is about the same as that of male high school graduates (approximately $25,187 and $26,045, respectively). There is also evidence that the wage gap increases the longer women remain continuously employed. A recent study analyzed the hourly earnings of women and men with 16 years or more of school and no work interruptions (i.e., continuously employed) for the year 1984 (U.S. Department of Labor, Women's Bureau, 1990b). Compared to men's earnings, women's earnings decreased from 86.2 cents per dollar for women 21 to 29 years of age to 73.9 cents per dollar for women 30 to 44 years of age. For women 45 to 64 years of age it dropped to 61 cents per each dollar earned by men.

Thus women continue to earn less than men, and few wives earn more than husbands. Of the 3.8 million individuals with incomes in excess of $75,000, 87% are male. Among dual-career heterosexual couples, approximately 20% of wives earn as much or more income, and 80% earn less than husbands. Lesbian women, like women in general, earn less than men on average, which means lower joint earnings as a couple than for heterosexual partners (Schneider, 1986). For gay male couples, in contrast, this fact means higher joint earnings (Hodnett, 1991). Overall, then, there are favorable indicators for increased gender parity, but heterosexual partners' presumed economic parity has yet to be achieved.

Assumption 2 concerns the compatibility of occupational and family systems. Here again the assumption is crucial to understanding how the dual-career family form holds out the promise of gender equality. Historically, individuals were assigned roles based on their sex. Women primarily cared for children and husbands, and whoever else needed care, and men provided the economic wherewithal for their various dependents. As society became more industrialized, the separation of work and family activities became more pronounced. Although many women worked, it was with the assumption that they held primary responsibility for the family's daily functioning and well-being. Pregnant women had no place in the work force, and most women with young children moved in and out of the workplace or stayed out of the work force altogether. Child care often was provided by family members or friends, although for women with more economic resources employed help was the norm.

The notion that a person, female or male, could pursue a career and actively be involved in family life simply was not an option one considered. The structures of career participation were built by men on the basis of being family-free (Fowlkes, 1987). Men's freedom to pursue careers came from having women in their lives to sustain their ambition and attend to the details of their lives. Freedom for women to pursue careers was achieved by avoiding "the marriage plot" and remaining outside of marriage and family altogether (Heilbrun, 1988).

The situation today differs in a number of significant ways. The Pregnancy Discrimination Act of 1978, for instance, prohibits discrimination on the basis of pregnancy, childbirth, or related medical conditions. Nearly all large employers provide for maternity leaves of 30 to 90 days, and many women with small children remain in the labor force. But as I discuss at length in Chapter 6 and later in this chapter, there is considerable resistance to altering the structure of occupational work, particularly professional work, and providing policies that assume women and men, not just women, involve themselves in family work. Paternity leaves, for example, pose unique difficulties for organizations because granting such leaves would sanction men as caregivers and alter firmly held views that families accommodate to the structure of men's work (Fowlkes, 1980, 1987). At the present time, Congress and the White House have yet to reach a compromise on federal family leave proposals although several states have passed legislation in this area (see Chapter 6 for more detail on this topic). This situation leaves the United States as one of the few major Western countries with no national policy for guaranteeing women or men the right to maternity or paternity leave, no job protection in the event of such a leave, no cash benefit to help compensate for not working due to childbirth, and no care for the newborn (Kamerman, 1988, 1991).

Achieving the occupational and familial compatibility implicit in assumption 2, then, requires changes that go far beyond what has been witnessed to date. Needed changes range from views of women's and men's capacities and roles, the nature of careers, and federal and state policies to a clear articulation of what brings meaning to women's and men's lives.

Assumption 3 pertains to the partners themselves and thus to aspects of dual-career family functioning over which the partners have relatively more direct control. Basically it was assumed that spouses' self-concepts as women and men allow for the establishment of a relationship characterized by role-sharing and mutuality and by an interdependency free of the constraints of gender. When we peruse the evidence pertinent to this assumption, which I do throughout the book, considerable variability emerges. Some heterosexual partners achieve what both they and others would characterize as an egalitarian, role-sharing relationship built around their own needs and priorities and the realities of their situation. Other dual-career relationships are far from egalitarian with wives doing significantly more of the household work and parenting than husbands and husbands working longer hours on the job than wives (Pleck, 1985; Thompson & Walker, 1989).

Reaching a conclusion about this third assumption is difficult because it is the most complex of the three to verify. Women and men act out their private roles as spouses, parents, and homemakers within the larger world of occupational and institutional structures and policies. Privately decided upon principles of equality may prove inconsistent with social institutions that embody the values of male authority over women.

Why things have changed so much yet in some crucial ways have stayed so much the same is the subject of much discussion and theorizing. Current thinking centers around the concept of gender as central to an explanatory theory for elucidating and explaining these processes. Particularly important in these theoretical discussions is the conceptual shift in the focus of sociopsychological inquiry from sex to gender and from gender as difference to gender as both organizer and process. Gender models move theorizing about dual-career families away from an emphasis on the individual behavior of women and men and toward a recognition of the "gendered" context in which individual behavior occurs, both today and in the past. Moreover, rather than positing two opposite, comprehensive, consistent, and exclusive "sex roles," the new theories identify a variety of actively gendered mechanisms that link individuals and families with other social institutions (Ferree, 1990). These models, then, clearly tie gender to social processes.

❧ Gender Theory

> It's the frames which makes some things important and some things forgotten. It's all only frames from which the content arises. (Babitz, 1979, p. 137)

The cultural, biological, and psychological questions about love, marriage, and the personal relations between women and men are inextricably tied to sex and gender. Earlier I mentioned the conceptual shift in the field of psychology that accompanied the preference for the term *gender,* rather than sex, in studying women's and men's personal and interpersonal behavior within a social context. This section describes recent thinking about this complex construct and explains how the preference for the term *gender* represents a fundamental change in how we think about women and men in relationships.

The term *gender* acknowledges the broader meaning typically associated with one's biological sex. Sherif (1982) described how biological sex forms the basis of a social classification system—namely, gender—in which many of the traits and behaviors traditionally associated with biological sex become "constructed by the social reality" of individual women and men (Hare-Mustin & Marecek, 1990). Thus, gender refers not only to biological sex, but also to the psychological, social, and cultural features and characteristics strongly associated with the biological categories of female and male (Deaux, 1985; Whiting & Edwards, 1988).

As Babitz noted, "It's the frames which make things important," and gender essentially provides different frames. Its frames are behaviors in gendered social environments, not biological-sex-determined behaviors devoid of social contexts. Rather than focusing on intrapsychic variables presumably tied to biological sex in order to explicate and elucidate human behavior, gender perspectives consider human behavior as emerging from a web of interactions between women's and men's biological being and their social environment. Two examples illustrate the difference:

> *Example 1.* Women and men in our society are equally likely to become parents (biologically, conception requires a female and a male), but disproportionately more women than men involve themselves in the day-to-day care of children. From a gender perspective, women typically rear children, not because men lack nurturing genes, but because societal expectations associated with sex prescribe that women, more than men, engage in nurturing activities (i.e., culturally, women rear children).

Example 2. This second example uses the statistics on education and earning power presented earlier. Young women and men today are equally likely to receive a college degree but on average men's starting salaries are higher. From a gender perspective, men earn more, not because they are more capable than women by nature, but because employment practices reward men more than women (i.e., culturally, men "provide").

What happens when one changes the frame of inquiry from an internally determined sex differences model to a broader contextual gender perspective? A case in point is women's stress in combining multiple roles. Earlier studies assumed the cause of the stress was the women themselves and primarily looked at intrapsychic variables such as guilt, self-esteem, and ambition. Later studies framed the personal experience of role conflict within the context of women's lives. By broadening the explanatory models researchers could correctly identify the importance of such contextual variables as spouse participation in family work, child-care availability and quality, and employers' policies to individual well-being and marital satisfaction (Crosby, 1987; Gilbert, 1988; Thompson & Walker, 1989).

Finally, the focus on the broader term *gender* led to a further articulation of the concept of gender itself. The subsections that follow describe the ways gender operates as difference, organizer or structure, and process.

Gender as Difference

In her book *The Man-Made World,* the writer Charlotte Gilman (1914) concluded that the 19th century had been "oversexed" in that the differences between the sexes were exaggerated. "That one sex should have monopolized all human activities, called them 'men's work,' and managed them as such, is what is meant by the phrase 'Androcentric culture' " (p. 25). Scholars in the natural and social sciences reached similar conclusions with regard to the nature of science (Keller, 1985) and prevalent biological (Fausto-Sterling, 1985) and psychological theories (Hare-Mustin & Marecek, 1990) about women and men.

Historically when researchers compared the behavior of women and men, it was often done with the assumption that the sexes were opposite and thus possessed non-overlapping attributes and abilities. Thus not only were many observed differences implicitly or explicitly attributed to biological sex, but also differences in magnitude often were interpreted as differences in kind (e.g., mean differences on responses to the rod and frame test resulted in labeling women as field dependent and men as field independent). Researchers such as Block (1984) questioned these assumptions and consequently investigated how implicit views about the sexes being opposite became manifest in parents' and teachers' views of and behaviors with girls and boys. The different sociocultural contexts experienced by girls and boys during childhood and adolescence became important to understanding such findings as girls' reports of greater math anxiety and boys' development of greater potency of self-concept (Eccles, 1987). Similarly, social patterns, such as women earning less than men in comparable positions and employed women with children experiencing greater role conflict than men, came to be understood as related to being female or male within a particular societal structure, and not to being female or male per se. In other words, such patterns came to be understood as gender differences, not sex differences.

The focus on gender differences clearly broadened our understanding of behavior in its social context. However, it also "obscured inequality" by masking the differences in power between women and men and, thus, the other ways in which gender operates in the culture (Hare-Mustin, 1991).

Gender as Organizer or Structure

Sherif (1982) also viewed gender as extending beyond individual women and men and their differential socialization to the social structures and principles of organizations. She argued that gender was a pervasive organizer in the society. Persistent, highly visible dynamics in the culture support her view.

Positions of power and leadership in business organizations and academic institutions still are held predominantly by men (Rix, 1987), and overall men have a wider base of power and easier access to valuable resources. Despite enormous gains, women still are greatly underrepresented in nearly all professional areas. Moreover, women experience significant attrition in male-dominated professions (Rix,

1987; U.S. Bureau of Labor Statistics, 1989). As surprising as it may sound, the occupational distribution of women within the labor force has changed only slightly over time: Women and men still are typically found in different occupations (Scott, 1982; Spain, 1988). Nursing, for example, remains 99% female and engineering, 94% male. Among secretaries, stenographers, and typists, 96% are women. Approximately one in four working women held a secretarial job in 1950, and approximately one in three now holds such a position. In 1989 women represented 80% of all administrative support (including clerical) workers but only about 9% of all precision, production, craft, and repair workers. Women were 68% of all retail and personal service sales workers, but only 40% of all executives, managers, and administrators (U.S. Department of Labor, Women's Bureau, 1990a). Finally, women continue to earn significantly less than men (U.S. Bureau of Labor Statistics, 1991).

How does gender as structure contribute to these findings? Factors imbedded in societal views of male superiority and the androcentrism described by Gilman become manifest as structural barriers to women's career development and advancement. For example, women today are experiencing the so-called glass ceiling, transparent but powerful artificial barriers based on attitudinal or organizational biases that keep women and minorities from advancing upward in their organization into management level positions (Cole, 1981; Morrison, White, Velsor, & Center for Creative Leadership, 1987; U.S. Department of Labor, 1991). In 1990 minorities and women held less than 5% of the top executive positions of our nation's 1,000 largest corporations, up from less than 3% in 1979. Also in 1990, women held only 4.5% of the directorships and 2.6% of the officer positions in the *Fortune* 500 companies (Lublin, 1991).

A study recently conducted by the U.S. Department of Labor (1991) found that the glass ceiling occurs far below middle management and appears early on in "pipelines to the top." The same stereotypes and misperceptions documented by researchers were found in companies' decisions and records. Women were simply assumed not to possess leadership qualities. Ironically, comprehensive meta-analytic studies on gender and leadership find no overall sex differences in leader effectiveness (Eagly, 1991). In fact, once studies with extreme findings are removed from the data, women are rated "somewhat more effective than men." Based on these and other findings, Eagly concluded that women do quite well in leadership roles and are at least as effective as their male counterparts.

A second example pertains to corporate policy and the recent controversy about the "mommy track." Felice Schwartz (1989), president of Catalyst, proposed a way to retain talented women in management and still allow women to manage the issues of parenting. (Catalyst is a national organization that has worked within the corporate community since 1962 to foster the full participation of women in business and professional life.) Schwartz proposed two tracks for young professional women entering organizations: a fast track, similar to the usual male track, for women who were not family-oriented, and a less demanding track (what the media labeled "the mommy track") for women who were. That a person as knowledgeable as Schwartz could propose separate tracks for women shocked many into seeing how corporate and personnel policy can maintain a male-dominant structure. Employed men with children are still viewed as men, but employed women with children are considered mothers. As this situation demonstrates, gender as organizer can profoundly affect the personal lives and interpersonal relations of spouses in dual-career families.

Gender as Interactive Process

Recent theorists also emphasize how gender is an interactive process engaged in by women and men (Deaux, 1984; Sherif, 1982; Unger, 1990). In this process, women and men internalize societally based constructions of women and men and are encouraged and rewarded for playing out those constructions in their interpersonal interactions—particularly in those kinds of interactions where gender is salient. Deaux (1984), in her review of a decade of work on gender, concluded that views of gender as a static category must give way to, or at least be accompanied by, theories that treat sex-related phenomena as a process—"a process that is influenced by individual choices, molded by situational pressures, and ultimately understandable only in the context of social interaction" (p. 115). The parallel conversations depicted in Figure 1.1 provide a humorous example of this process. In negotiating a time to get together the woman plan around possible times with men but the men just decide.

Figure 1.1. Getting Together With a Close Friend. . . a Tale of Two Genders

The work of Eccles and her colleagues provides additional examples. Their studies demonstrate how parents' gender-related expectations influence children's participation in gender-role stereotyped activities such as mathematics and sports (Eccles, Jacobs, & Harold, 1990). Essentially parents' expectancies distort perceptions of and attributions for their own children's competencies and interests (e.g., daughters' good grades come from working hard and sons' from being good at math), and these in turn influence the child's self-perceptions and activity choices (e.g., his or her self-efficacy in math).

Similar processes occur in educational environments. Reasons for women's serious underrepresentation in science and engineering, for example, center around internalized sexist attitudes about women's abilities and roles that are communicated to students from an early age (AAUW, 1991). Ongoing interactions with professors and peers communicate negative judgments of women's academic abilities, yet inundate women with social attention. Exclusionary practices keep female students out of informal networks, and the risk of attracting romantic attention may keep them out of mentoring relationships with professors, nearly all of whom are male (Brush, 1991).

Parallel dynamics occur in work settings. Interpersonal processes based on assumed or unconsciously held views of gender-related characteristics, such as male superiority, may maintain interpersonal dynamics that keep men in dominant positions they may not even want. The studies by Eagly and her colleagues were previously mentioned. People in authority assume men outperform women despite data to the contrary (Eagly, 1991). A series of studies with college students indicated that under certain situational constraints women, even those who are high in dispositional dominance, might accept the legitimacy of men's assumed power or status and then act in accordance with this assumption (Davis & Gilbert, 1989). More specifically, these authors found that high dominant women paired with low dominant men became leader 71% of the time. However, high dominant women paired with high dominant men assumed the leadership role only 31% of the time. Thus, men's expectancies may be a more important determinant of interaction sequences in mixed-sex dyads than are women's, and women in mixed-sex dyads may inadvertently confirm men's behavioral expectancies more than men confirm women's (e.g., Davis & Gilbert, 1989).

Finally, the dynamics underlying sexual harassment have to do with these same kinds of gender processes (Chapter 2 discusses sexual discrimination in some detail). As Catharine MacKinnon (1979) noted in her ground-breaking book *Sexual Harassment of Working Women*, "sexual harassment has not only been legally allowed, it has also been legally unthinkable" (p. xi). Behaviors that we now know constitute sexual harassment only 10 years ago were so much a part of the social order, so customary and agreeing with traditional views of how women and men interact in environments where men had more power, they were invisible.

As these illustrations make clear, individuals engage in behaviors prompted by gender-related beliefs and constraints, and they do so much more often than realized. Chapters 2 and 3 further explain how gender processes influence personal and work relationships, both directly and indirectly. Views of men as superior to women and entitled, sexually and otherwise, continue to influence employers' policies and practices as well as women's and men's self-views

Table 1.1 Summary of a Comparison of Earlier and Current Views of Sex and Gender

---

Example 1: Women are more emotionally expressive than men.

Interpretation Based on Sex as an Internal Determiner: By nature women are emotional and men are not.

Interpretation From a Contextual Gender Perspective: *Gender as difference*—women more than men are encouraged by the society to self-disclose feelings and emotions.

Example 2: Women cluster in the helping and service professions and men cluster in business, sciences, and higher education.

Interpretation Based on Sex as an Internal Determiner: Women prefer positions involving nurturing activities.

Interpretation From a Contextual Gender Perspective: *Gender as structure*—corporate and institutional policies and practices serve to keep women and men in female- and male-dominated occupations, respectively.

Example 3: Women underfunction in relationships with men.

Interpretation Based on Sex as an Internal Determiner: Women need men.

Interpretation From a Contextual Gender Perspective: *Gender as interactive process*—when one sex is dependent on the other it will endeavor for safety's sake to simulate what the dominant sex finds desirable. In our society this results in women and men unconsciously engaging in processes that keep men entitled.

---

and expectations. Realities such as the underrepresentation of women in most professional areas and the inequities in men's and women's salaries perpetuate societal views of, and sanctions for, male dominance.

Table 1.1 presents a summary of the various aspects of gender just described and how interpretations from this perspective differ from those based on sex as an internal determiner. Clearly these three ways of thinking about gender processes are highly correlated and mutually influencing, as depicted in Figure 1.2. For example, views of women as nurturers and men as providers become associated with their respective abilities and "rightful place" in the workplace (gender as organizer or structure) and with internalized views women and men bring to interactions (gender as interactional process).

Studies of the Dual-Career Family

Not surprisingly, research on the dual-career family initially focused on women's changing roles and then on comparisons of women

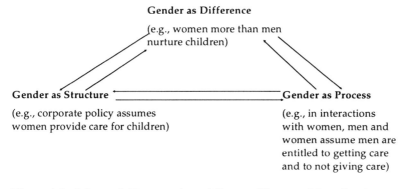

Gender as Difference

(e.g., women more than men nurture children)

Gender as Structure

(e.g., corporate policy assumes women provide care for children)

Gender as Process

(e.g., in interactions with women, men and women assume men are entitled to getting care and to not giving care)

Figure 1.2. Schematic Presentation of Current Views on How Gender Operates in the Society and Culture

and men. Hence, a good deal of the research reported in later chapters was conceptualized, implicitly or explicitly, from a gender-as-difference perspective. Many studies, for example, compare husbands and wives on such variables as satisfaction, self-esteem, expressivity, and participation in family work. The gender-as-difference approach also implicitly guided investigations of phenomena assumed to be associated with one partner but not the other. For instance, although women's changing roles outside the home alter both spouses' roles within the home, women are studied more often than men, although much less so today than in the past. A related example is the extensive literature on the effects of maternal employment on children. Only recently have researchers broadened their views of parenting to study the effects of paternal employment (Hoffman, 1989).

Topics discussed in later chapters also relate to gender as structure (e.g., family benefits) and gender as interactive process (e.g., participation in family work). Studies that conceptualize gender as structure appear with increasing frequency in the literature. Pleck (1990), for example, is interested in how employer policies regarding paternity leave influence men's participation in parenting. Similarly, Hyde and Clark (1988) are investigating the relationship between maternity leave options and family members' well-being (see also Hyde & Essex, 1991). Few studies, however, directly address gender as interactive process, although throughout the book I discuss topics pertinent to this area such as power, participation in family work, and decision making about locating and relocating.

⋈ Summary

This chapter describes the emergence of the two-career family form and how, in theory, it represents dramatic social change and holds the promise of gender equality. Pertinent data are presented about the experiences of women and men in educational and employment settings—data that reflect a vastly different social climate for young adults today than for their parents just 20 years earlier. The past two decades witnessed enormous changes in women's and men's behavior. The choices of young adults today, unlike those of many of their parents, will occur within the broader framework of combining occupational work and family rather than of precluding one or the other. Nonetheless, traditional gender processes continue to operate at all levels in our society, from stereotypes and belief systems to interpersonal ways of behaving, social structures, and organizations. In the next chapter I describe and illustrate the myriad ways in which gender profoundly affects women's lives. In Chapter 3 I then describe the effects on men.

2

❦

Contemporary Female Perspectives

A poignant cartoon depicts a professional-looking couple contemplating the purchase of a book. The woman says to the man, "It's by a woman who still thinks marriage is possible" (Hamilton, 1983).

This is not the first time women have questioned whether relationships with men were possible given the societal structure and its explicit and implicit norms and policies. Lucy Stone and Henry Blackwell, early U.S. feminists, at the time of their wedding in 1855, publicly announced their intent to live their private lives outside the institutional constraints of the time. They said:

> While we acknowledge our mutual affection by publicly assuming the relationship of husband and wife . . . we deem it a duty to declare that this act on our part implies no sanction of, nor promise of voluntary obedience to such of the present laws of marriage as refuse to recognize the wife as an independent, rational being, while they confer upon

the husband an injurious and unnatural superiority. (Flexner, 1959, p. 64)

Husbands in the United States no longer have custody of the wife's person, yet the issues of male dominance and superiority and female obedience and dependency identified in the Stone-Blackwell statement persist today—some 100 years later—and profoundly influence women's and men's self-concepts and choices. Hare-Mustin (1991), a keen observer of gender processes, recently concluded that "Women live under the kind of patriarchy that is represented, not by outright oppression, but by the unacknowledged preeminence of men's desires and the subordination of their own" (p. 56).

Combining careers and personal relations presents different practical, psychological, and social issues for women and men. That is why women more than men push for dual-career marriages, despite the lack of equality at home and work, and why, when resistances emerge, women more than men accommodate. This chapter and the next identify powerful gender processes so customary and familiar they often go unrecognized by women and men alike, and cause difficulties to dual-career relationships as a result.

I again start with the broader perspective and look briefly at women's history with regard to careers and personal relationships. Next, two powerful gender dynamics in our society, dependency and personal achievement, are analyzed from the viewpoint of the female experience. In parallel fashion, Chapter 3 then considers the male side of these gender dynamics.

✿ Women's Changing History

Women have served all these centuries as looking glasses possessing the magic and delicious power of reflecting the figure of man at twice its natural size. (Woolf, 1929/1957, p. 35)

To a large degree women have been conditioned to focus their lives around men. For centuries women accommodated to men's needs, regardless of their own talents and abilities. Their efforts to act autonomously and to broaden their interests beyond the sphere of the family were met with great skepticism mostly because such actions ran counter to "women's nature." Moreover, as Woolf indicated in the introductory quotation, women also gave strength to men. They reflected back to men what men needed to sustain their ambitions, achieve their goals, and maintain their sense of self as a man. Perhaps the clearest literary example of this is provided by Woolf (1927/1955) herself in the novel *To the Lighthouse,* when she describes the relationship between Mr. and Mrs. Ramsey.

> He wanted sympathy. He was a failure, he said. Mrs. Ramsey flashed her needles. Mr. Ramsey repeated, never taking his eyes from her face, that he was a failure. She blew the words back at him. . . . It was sympathy he wanted, to be assured of his genius, first of all, and then to be taken within the circle of life, warmed and soothed, to have his senses restored to him, his barrenness made fertile, and all of the rooms of the house made full of life. . . . She assured him, beyond a shadow of a doubt, by her laugh, her poise, her competence, that it was real; the house was full. If he put implicit faith in her, nothing should hurt him; however deep he buried himself or climbed high. . . . Mrs. Ramsey felt not only exhausted in body (afterwards, not at the time, she always felt this) but also there tinged her physical fatigue some faintly disagreeable sensation with another origin. . . . It came from this: she did not like, even for a second, to feel finer than her husband; and further, could not bear not being entirely sure, when she spoke to him, of the truth of what she said. (Woolf, 1927/1955, pp. 58-62)

Thus Mr. Ramsey believes himself brilliant and independent and Mrs. Ramsey uses her strength to maintain this illusion, for not even she could bear the thought of him not being stronger and wiser than her.

Young adults today may not realize how recently women have had the freedom to develop their own lives and how fragile that freedom may be. Women today are creating their own narratives for the first time. In her book *Writing a Woman's Life,* Heilbrun (1988) reminds us: "Women have long been nameless. They have not been persons. Handed by a father to another man, the husband, they have been objects for circulation, exchanging one name for another" (p. 121). In literary works, as in real life, death and marriage were the only two possible ends for women, and were frequently the same end—for the young woman ceased to be an entity, a person in her own right.

Women were to have no life apart from their husbands and families. Ibsen (1879/1959) poignantly brought this to our attention in *A Doll's House.* Nora's husband, Torvald, tells her that her most sacred duty is to her husband and children. She responds:

Nora: I have other duties just as sacred.
Torvald: That you have not. What duties could those be?
Nora: Duties to myself.
Torvald: Before all else, you are a wife and a mother.
Nora: I don't believe that any longer. I believe that before all else I am a reasonable human being, just as you are—or at all events, that I must try to become one. I know quite well, Torvald, that most people would think you right, and that views of that kind are to be found in books; but I can no longer content myself with what most people say, or with what is found in books. I must think over things for myself and get to understand them.

(Ibsen, 1879/1959, p. 65)

Women, like Nora, who sought self-definition typically had to do so outside of the institution of marriage. This fact remains somewhat true today. Tradition and patriarchy pressure women to choose between career and family and to keep caregiving as a personal, female domain. As I discuss later, women more than men worry about how to combine work and family and alter career goals and paths to accommodate this eventuality.

Women's growing freedom of self-definition brings with it increased opportunity for women (and men) and increased risk and confusion. Some young women feel overwhelmed by the lack of role models and clear paths to follow. Others question how real, how secure their new freedom is. Can relationships with men be negotiated without women finding themselves giving up their life to the relationship? Can work and family be negotiated by partners who hold egalitarian values, if the larger society still sees women and men as fundamentally different and men as superior?

❧ Women, Relationships, and Careers

"Possible selves," according to Markus and Nurius (1986), represent individuals' ideas of what they might become, what they would like to become, and what they are afraid of becoming. Theoretically individuals could create any number of possible selves. In actuality the set of possible selves derives from individuals' experiences within their particular sociocultural and historical context and the models, images, and symbols that that culture provides them. Possible selves reveal the uniqueness of the self to the extent that the self is not socially determined and constrained.

An individual's possible selves regarding occupational work and family develop in the context of societal views about women's and men's abilities and the structural opportunities for, or constraints on, the expression of relevant behaviors and goals (Gilbert & Dancer, 1992). Images of possible selves guide short-term and long-term educational, occupational, and relational goals. The gender-related concepts of dependency and personal achievement, discussed next, particularly influence women's and men's images of what they can possibly be.

Love and the Construction
of Female Dependency

"Most Americans have an incomplete, feminine conception of love" (Cancian, 1987, p. 69). Cancian argues that the feminine conception of love, which involves emotional expression and talking about feelings, exaggerates the difference between women's and men's ability to love and their need for love. In her view, it also reinforces men's power advantage and encourages women to overspecialize in relationships, whereas men overspecialize in work.

That women need men more than men need women is likely a universal view. Women long have depended on men for their sense of self and were willing to be led and spoken for by men. Men defined women's capacities and characteristics and, on this basis, made judgments about women's optimal functioning and goals in educational and occupational settings and in the private sphere. Recall Nora's words in Ibsen's *A Doll's House*, written in 1879: "I know most people agree with you, Torvald, and that's also what it says in books. But I'm not content any more with what most people say, or with what it says in books."

The idea that woman's nature was to serve men represented the patriarchal ideal of womanhood. Simone de Beauvoir (1970) observed that "One is not born, one rather becomes a woman" (p. 249). Men's position of power over women assured men's relative superiority. It benefitted men to perceive women as primarily longing to love a man, to admire him and serve him, and even to pattern herself after him. Male characteristics became the ideal for women and men alike although women could never attain these characteristics in their own right. Freud (1933) concluded, for example, that where a woman's choice of a man is able to show itself freely, it is often made in accordance with the narcissistic ideal of the man whom she had wished to become.

Women were primarily considered in relation to men. Rarely was it asked, "What are women for themselves?" Woman as subject, as a creator of personal drama, was unthinkable. Women were objects in other people's dramas and had no personal story, no separateness from the fabric of men's lives. "For this reason, then, women who began to write another story often wrote it under another name. They were inventing something so daring they could not risk, in their own person, the frightful consequences" (Heilbrun, 1988, p. 121).

Despite changes in women's status, the legacy of women's dependency remains strong in contemporary depictions of women and in the minds of many women and men as well. Popular books remind us that either "women love too much" or are desperate for men. *Fringe Benefits* (Gates, 1989) tells us the company benefit of most interest to women is the proportion of "eligible" men. The author assumes, and perhaps correctly, that women prefer as marital partners men who are smarter, more mature, better educated, and better paid. The February 1989 issue of *Cosmopolitan* magazine told women "How to attract a man like crazy." And the more educated a woman, the more desperate the depiction (Faludi, 1991). I wonder how long the cartoon strip "Cathy" can last. Every day it reminds us that single career women obsess about getting a man, controlling their eating, and maintaining their beauty.

Historically, being valued and desired by men was an important component of a woman's self-concept because women's worth to men was seen in terms of their physical characteristics and their ability to please, satisfy, and serve men (Westkott, 1986). One result of these gendered processes is what Brehm (1988) described as women's need to discover themselves through the reactions of others, particularly men. According to Brehm, because women still gain status and meaning through connections with men, they have internalized a specific hunger for male approval that serves to inhibit their own self-definition.

One consequence of these realities is women's overevaluating the importance of relationships and looking to relationships as a way to feel important or worthwhile (Heilbrun, 1988; Lerner, 1983; Westkott, 1986). Still today many women are socialized to believe that being partnered or married is a first priority in life and that achieving financial independence and career recognition are secondary to their roles as caregivers and partners. In heterosexual relationships this is further complicated by the status historically associated with being loved by a man and the promise of being taken care of financially and otherwise. Women's lives being given meaning through their attachment to men and men taking care of women in return remain powerful metaphors for women and men today. Being without a man supposedly means the woman is undesirable and unlovable, a belief that can bring about feelings of shame and inadequacy, despite a woman's career accomplishments.

Educated in Romance: Women, Achievement, and College Culture (Holland & Eisenhart, 1990) provides a particularly relevant illustration of this process in college-aged women and men attending two southern universities in the late 1980s. The authors detail how institutional practices and informal networks reinforce women's scaling down their career aspirations. A woman's status becomes tied to phone calls, popularity, and demands by men for exclusivity, and not to academic performance. A particularly dramatic finding was the number of women who narrowed their professional and personal options once they had a boyfriend. These findings fit with those of other researchers and with our findings. Two illustrations come to mind. The first concerns a talented young woman who decided to forgo her last year of college to join her boyfriend who was graduating and moving to another city: "I can finish my degree at any time, so why risk the relationship?" Another young woman was amazed at how easy it was for her to devote most of her first two years in college to a relationship that was not very satisfying: "I was overwhelmed by the university and unsure of my abilities; having a boyfriend kept me from having to confront my own insecurities."

These stories of declining female ambition sound more like the 1950s than the 1980s and thus attest to the enduring power of gender in shaping women's and men's lives. Not surprisingly, career identities are less likely to erode among young women who do not rush into intimate heterosexual relationships in high school and college. Indeed, women who enter professional fields typically marry after completing advanced degrees and start families after careers are established.

Lerner (1983) observed a similar dynamic in female-male interactions that she identified as "female underfunctioning." To attract and hold on to men, women may take on dependent stances with men, which in turn require that they somehow subordinate themselves to men. Women may play down their intellectual ability and their professional ambition, for example, and put a greater emphasis on their physical beauty and attractiveness. The underfunctioning serves to protect men from the knowledge that these women may be smarter or more capable than the men and to protect women from the rejection such knowledge would bring.

Fiction and literary allusion sometimes reveal truths that reality obscures, so again I turn to literature to illustrate my point. A 1937 poem by Stevie Smith describes the cost to women who do or do not assume dependent stances with men.

> Marriage I think
> For women
> Is the best of opiates.
> It kills the thoughts
> That think about the thoughts,
> It is the best of opiates.
> So said Maria.
> But too long in solitude she'd dwelt,
> And too long her thoughts had felt
> Their strength. So when the man drew near,
> Out popped her thoughts and covered him with fear.
> Poor Maria!
> Better that she had kept her thoughts on a chain,

For now she's alone again and all in pain;
She sighs for the man that went and the thoughts that stay
To trouble her dreams by night and her dreams by day.

(Barbara & McBrien, 1981, p. 216)

In *Backlash: The Undeclared War Against American Women,* Faludi (1991) details how journalists played up "the frightful consequences" of women's self-definition, and how vulnerable women were to their message: "Career-minded women end up without a man." Truly successful women attach to or affiliate with men and do all that is necessary to make that happen. Containing or limiting their own achievement or assuming a dependent stance may become necessary if relationships with men become endangered.

I have never had a man come into my office worried about being too competent or too self-assured, but many women have. They describe struggles with the negative reactions they receive from male peers, professors, and employers for showing their knowledge or challenging the ideas of others. Women who do not need men's approval, women who make choices separate from the needs of men, women who are no more and no less capable than men on average are frightening—to women and men alike. Recall the uproar caused by the film *Thelma and Louise.* Perhaps most revealing was a cartoon by Steve Kelley (1991). It depicted two men coming out of a movie theater. One says to the other, "It should've been rated PMS . . ." When women get too threatening—for example, by not needing men or by refusing to live within the parameters set by men—we attribute their behavior to raging hormones beyond their control rather than to rational thought and willful action.

In summary, traditional beliefs about female dependency and women's relational nature pervade our society. This reality may cause female and male partners, consciously or unconsciously, to frame their experiences in stereotypic ways. Unwittingly they may interpret their behaviors as reinforcing the notion that women prefer to live their lives through men (and their children) rather than seeing these acts as tied to the social processes of gender and power that shape women's and men's lives.

Rewards, Costs, and Barriers
to Personal Achievement

We now know that, contrary to stereotype, women's and men's cognitive abilities are highly similar (Fausto-Sterling, 1985; Feingold, 1988; Hyde, 1991). There is also evidence that women perform better than men in college as reflected in higher grades in their major field and taking less time to complete their degrees (U.S. Department of Education, 1991). The first chapter mentioned the increasing percentages of women entering law, medicine, and business. In 1960, one female college student in two received her degree in teaching; today business surpasses teaching as a field of study, with 45% of bachelor of arts degrees in business earned by women.

Personal achievement invariably benefits men in our culture. Is the same true for women? Despite women's greater access to educational opportunities and their performing as well as men educationally, women receive fewer rewards in the labor market. Differences in salary and promotion rates were detailed in Chapter 1. Women with five or more years of college, working full-time, make only 69 cents for every dollar earned by men. Relatively few women have broken through the glass ceiling.

The discussions on female dependency suggest that women's possible selves may be particularly susceptible to societal pressures to attach to men, which, in turn, would place constraints on images of personal achievement. Miller (1991), in her book *Seductions*, explores the reasons that educated women of this century allowed men to exclude women from intellectual life and then to collude with male theorists' views of women. Many women today find the courage to resist collusion, despite its comforts, and to say what they think or feel, despite "the frightful consequences." And they do this despite realities that work against women's self-development.

What follows is a brief discussion of external or structural factors that constrain women's personal achievement. Not all women experience these factors and not all women who experience them become daunted. Nonetheless these factors remain part of the female experience today.

Educational experiences. Adrienne Rich's (1979) essay "Taking Women Students Seriously" instructs us:

> Listen to the small, soft voices, often courageously trying to speak
> up, voices of women taught early that tones of confidence, challenge,
> anger, or assertiveness, are strident and unfeminine. Listen to the voices
> of the women and the voices of the men; observe the space men allow
> themselves, physically and verbally, the male assumption that people
> will listen, even when the majority of the group is female. (p. 243)

Women today are taken more seriously as students and scholars
than in early times, but likely not seriously enough. Research indicates that compared to male peers, young women today develop
less confidence in their capabilities and believe less in their ability
to successfully perform in a chosen career. "Confident at 11, Confused
at 16" characterizes recent findings (AAUW, 1991; Prose, 1990). Girls,
aged 8 and 9, as a group are confident, assertive, and feel authori-
tative about themselves. By 15 or 16 the findings show much less
confidence and lowered self-esteem, compared to male peers. Such
beliefs affect women's "possible selves" with regard to individual
achievement—not only the professional life one envisions but also
persistence in achieving what one envisions.

Short-Changing Girls, Short-Changing America (AAUW, 1991) summarizes the results of a nationwide survey designed to assess self-
esteem, educational experiences, interest in science and mathematics,
and career aspirations of girls and boys, aged 9 to 15. Key findings
from the 3,000 black, hispanic, and white students surveyed were
the gender differences in self-esteem and the indication that girls
emerge from adolescence with a much poorer self-image, more constrained views of the future and their place in society, and much less
confidence in their abilities in comparison to their male peers. The
loss of self-confidence in girls, as they move from childhood to adolescence, was particularly dramatic. Possible reasons for these differential outcomes are considered in *How Schools Short-Change Girls,* a
comprehensive report for educators and policy makers on the educational experiences of girls from early childhood through grade 12
(AAUW, 1992). Consistent with gender stereotyping, the report indicated that classroom teachers give significantly more attention and
esteem-building encouragement to boys than to girls, that images
of women as contributors to knowledge still are marginalized or
ignored in textbooks and classroom activities, and that sexual harassment of girls by boys was an accepted practice.

Earlier research concluded that a "chilly classroom climate" still exists for high-achieving women. As a result of negative attitudes and judgments of women, educators use exclusionary practices, intellectual intimidation, or simply not noticing women's contributions in order to make women feel unwelcome and unworthy. Lowered self-comfort and self-confidence can result. Disproportionate numbers of women in leadership positions today attended women's colleges, suggesting that women's colleges provide a favorable climate for intellectually motivated female students (Tidball, 1989). Mills College, a women's school in Oakland, California, made headlines in 1990 when alumnae and students intensely opposed a decision by the trustees of the college to admit men. The women cogently argued that the environment of a coeducational college is hostile to women who seek to excel academically. The trustees reversed their decision.

Another area in which gender processes may put women at a disadvantage is mentoring. Through mentoring individuals develop a vision for themselves as well as the self-confidence to live these visions and to create new ones as needed. Mentoring processes also provide the kinds of knowledge, contacts, and experiences necessary for developing and extending one's educational and career options (Kram, 1988). Although mentoring involves a relationship between two people, the relationship itself occurs within and is maintained and influenced by the roles and norms of the relevant social systems and institutional structures (Gilbert & Rossman, 1992).

Consistent with statistics presented in the first chapter is the fact that most mentors today are still male. Men predominantly hold the positions of power and leadership in academic institutions and business organizations in which young women and men are educated and employed. Thus, many women still must look to men for mentoring and most mentor-protégé dyads are male-male or male-female.

This situation can be problematic for women. Male mentors may be harder to manage and provide a narrower range of benefits for women than for men (Morrison & Glinow, 1990). Mentors, for instance, may inadvertently fail to take into account the differential impact of educational or organizational practices and structure on female and male protégés, such as negative views of women, sexual harassment, and other forms of gender discrimination. Moreover, male mentors who do not concern themselves with integrating work and family life may lack experiences and skills in areas that likely do or will affect female protégés more than male. Mentors also may be unaware of their own dissimilar treatment of female and male protégés. It may be difficult and perhaps even threatening to use the mentoring relationship to empower female students and employees and help them create "daring images" of themselves as achieving women. A recent study of female executives, for example, indicated that most (71%) had a boss who helped their careers, and nearly all (91%) had one who hurt their careers (Fuchsberg, 1992). Careers were hindered or hurt mostly by male bosses described by such terms as "abusive, exploitative, hostile, sexist, and racist."

Because the cross-sex dyad is highly visible within organizations, male mentors may hold higher standards for women than men. In addition, apprehensions that close male-female working relationships automatically become sexualized in the minds of peers and supervisors, regardless of any indications to the contrary, may make men in positions to mentor reluctant to develop mentoring relationships with women. Ample evidence also indicates that male mentors assume they can enter into sexual relations with their protégés, a practice that reflects the legitimacy of male sexual dominance of women. Keller and Moglen (1987) indicated that younger women students seeking avenues to success "were sometimes asked to buy them with their bodies—from the males who agreed to be their mentors" (p. 496).

In summary, although women increasingly are being empowered educationally and occupationally, certain practices and processes in educational institutions continue to inhibit and undermine the development of women's personal achievement. These subtle processes must be understood and recognized as barriers to women's self-development.

Sexual harassment and other forms of gender discrimination. In a recent court decision, the male judge found the defendant not guilty of sexual harassment because the female plaintiff was "plain." This judge failed to see that sexual harassment is about power and the need to dominate, not physical attraction (Gutek, 1986, 1989; MacKinnon, 1979).

Sexual harassment, most broadly defined, refers to the unwanted imposition of sexual requirements in the context of unequal power. Many men hold an unconscious view that they are superior to women and that women should accommodate to men's needs. Sexual harassment in occupational settings occurs in many forms—innuendo, "friendly harassment," overt sexual comments, or even sexual coercion. In friendly harassment, "It's the daily little insults that wear you down." Male co-workers take the boys-will-be-boys attitude and expect their female co-workers to go along with their jokes about women's sexuality, their pin-ups in the office, their pinches, and lewd remarks. Still today, few women sexually harass men. In fact, studies indicate that many men think they would be flattered if their female boss or colleagues pressured them for dates or sexual favors (Verba, 1983). Clearly the meaning of such behaviors differs for men. They see as flattering what women experience as threatening; men think they would attribute to their own attractiveness what women experience as being about their "place" in society. I know of a woman who complained about a boss who put his hands on her breast and said, "Small but nice." Her boss thought the complaint was out of line. Yet I wonder how flattered a man would be if a female co-worker or superior put her hand on his genitals and said, "Small but nice."

A female neurosurgeon made the headlines not too long ago when she resigned (but later was convinced to reconsider) from the Stanford Medical School because of a quarter century of subtle sexism. She thought things were different for young women today, but reports from her students made her realize that women continue to suffer the same stream of insults in the medical school environment that she had experienced for the past 20 years (Barringa, 1991).

The preconfirmation hearings on charges that now Supreme Court Justice Clarence Thomas sexually harassed his former aide Anita Hill riveted our attention for weeks in the fall of 1991. Discussions following the hearings made clear that harassment remains a common workplace experience for women. Sexually suggestive remarks, unwanted touching, and behaviors and attitudes that demean or exclude women pervade the work environment. In the past women were expected to, and did, absorb the various forms of harassment for a variety of reasons—fear of reporting it to others in the work environment, blaming themselves for the attention or for not handling the situation better, fear they would not be believed or taken seriously.

The personal and professional costs to women who absorb and ignore their harassment are likely to be enormous. Assaults to self-esteem may be the most damaging (Bateson, 1990). The laws supposedly support women in this situation: "Legally, women are not arguably entitled, for example, to a marriage free of sexual harassment, nor are women legally guaranteed the freedom to walk down the street or into a court of law without sexual innuendo. In employment, the government promises more" (MacKinnon, 1979, p. 7). In reality, proof of sexual harassment may be difficult to come by, and women remain fearful of being labeled troublemakers or of accusations boiling down to "her word against his."

In 1986, the Supreme Court clarified its definition of sexual harassment to include subtle forms of intimidation—lingering, repeated sexual innuendos or comments—that create a "hostile environment" and unreasonably interfere with an individual's performance. Later, state courts ruled that any verbal or physical behavior that a "reasonable woman" would regard as offensive is covered by the law. These rulings are major steps because they move beyond blatant acts to the kinds of subtle, insidious attitudes and behaviors that undermine women's confidence and self-esteem. The "reasonable woman" perspective legitimizes women's perceptions and acknowledges that the meaning of behavior can differ because of gender processes. Conduct that many men consider unobjectionable, from their vantage point, many women find offensive and demeaning.

I mention sexual harassment not to scare women or blame men, but to point up an important dynamic in the workplace that impacts partners in dual-career families at many levels. Women and men must learn to recognize sexual harassment and sex discrimination and become informed about what to do should they themselves or their partner become a target. Recent prevalence figures suggest that 53% of women have been harassed at some point in their working lives, and about 10% have quit a job because of sexual harassment (Gutek, 1989). Women in nontraditional jobs are especially likely to be harassed (Rose & Larwood, 1988). Like other forms of gender discrimination, this is a phenomenon with which men are not necessarily personally familiar. In heterosexual couples, male partners may become educated about sexual harassment and become a source of support for their spouse. In addition, a supportive spouse may make it easier for women to confront harassing situations. However, in lesbian couples, where both partners may have to deal with harassment as well as homophobia, it may be harder for partners to confront the harassment dynamics and harder for them to leave a hostile work environment because of economics.

Sexual harassment and sex discrimination also are tied to extant beliefs about women already discussed. Perhaps most salient among these are the interrelated views that achievement is not "feminine" and that women cannot successfully combine families and careers. Some view women who desire careers and families as greedy and selfish. Others view them as destroying the nuclear family and displacing men at work. In the past, many women reconciled their achievement desires and societal views of women by choosing female-dominated occupations, not expecting to advance in their careers, or finding ways other than paid employment to use their talents and abilities.

Finally, less talked about is still another form of discrimination, namely, homophobia and heterosexism. Homophobia is the irrational fear, intolerance, and, in its most severe form, hatred of people who are gay or lesbian (Pharr, 1988). This type of prejudice leads to persistent beliefs in negative stereotypes toward gays and lesbians, and supports discriminating actions against these groups in areas such as jobs, housing, and child custody. Lesbians and gays, socialized in the same values, often internalize these negative stereotypes and develop some degree of self-hatred or low self-esteem, a form of internalized homophobia (Margolies, Becker, & Jackson-Brewer, 1987).

When homophobia is combined with cultural and institutional power, the result is heterosexism: a belief in the inherent superiority of heterosexuality and its right to dominance. This is analogous to sexist and racist attitudes, which, when combined with the cultural and institutional power to enforce these attitudes, result in sexism and racism. Heterosexism can have a powerful influence on a woman's (or man's) choice to envision, enter, or stay in a dual-career relationship with a same-sex partner. Being "out" on the job can have devastating repercussions for career advancement or even the right to remain employed. Yet choosing to "be discreet" also can have personal costs in terms of feeling isolated, compartmentalized, and unaffirmed.

In summary, although there are many reasons to be optimistic, much needs to be done before women will have a comparable place with men in the workplace and will be treated with the same respect and dignity. Later chapters discuss how this gendered reality influences processes between partners in dual-career families.

?? Summary

There is a long history of women having little authority and depending on others for their sense of self. Personal ambition was antithetical to what made women desirable and worthwhile. Although the experiences of Mrs. Ramsey and Nora are far removed from those of contemporary women, women today who put their own needs first or who call attention to their accomplishments still are suspect.

The complex relationship between female dependency, male dominance, and women's personal achievement plays out in different ways for heterosexual women. Recall the cartoon caption that opened the chapter: "It's by a woman who still thinks marriage is possible." Women may feel they have to choose between a career and marriage or accommodate to a husband. If the male partner is unwilling to engage in an egalitarian relationship, the woman may view the choice as one between equality and marriage. Indeed the literature indicates that many women find themselves doing more than their share and resenting it, and at the same time feeling reluctant to challenge male dominance and privilege because they fear losing the relationship or feel less competent and assured than the male partner (Gilbert, 1988). To maintain the dual-career family, these women may underfunction professionally as a way to subordinate their career desires to their partner's plans and aspirations (Lerner, 1983).

Early in the chapter the eloquent words of Stone and Blackwell (Flexner, 1959) described how, in a patriarchal society, both sexes are socialized to believe that men are more valuable than women and that men are entitled to many rights and privileges that are attendant to that fact. Men learn to see themselves as special and superior, and they learn to expect women to serve them. They are conditioned to assume that their needs and desires come before the needs and desires of women. Clearly, such beliefs are not likely to be consciously held by individuals envisioning dual-career relationships. Nonetheless feelings of entitlement may surface regarding how to perform domestic or parenting roles, whose career is primary, or who should make the larger salary. Male entitlement issues remain a struggle for men and women as they try to develop careers in a society that remains sexist and to form relationships that have little historical precedence. I now turn to the male side of things.

3

❦

Contemporary Male Perspectives

Two professional-looking men are conversing; one says to the other, "Men are coming back." (Cline, 1985)

The feminist movements of the 1960s and 1970s brought attention to how sexism oppresses women. How patriarchy harms men became a theme of the 1980s, and continues into the 1990s. Widely read books by men for men include: *The Hazards of Being Male: Surviving the Myth of Masculine Privilege* (Goldberg, 1976), *The Myth of Masculinity* (Pleck, 1981a), *How Men Feel: The Response to Women's Demands for Equality and Power* (Astrachan, 1986), *The Male Experience* (Doyle, 1989), *Men's Lives* (Kimmel & Messner, 1989), and most recently Robert Bly's *Iron John* (1991). Some writers, such as Goldberg and to some degree Bly, deny that men are privileged or that men dominate women. Rather, they see men as oppressed and burdened by their provider role, which cuts men off from their deeper selves and from bonding with and getting nurturing from other men. Other theorists, such as Pleck, Kimmel, and Doyle, believe men and women must be liberated from restricted gender roles that limit both sexes to less than full lives. Because masculinity is culturally created, not biologically mandated, they argue for structural changes that allow men to be nurturing and caring partners and parents as well as economic providers.

Despite the differences in emphasis and philosophy, these contemporary writers agree that the traditional system of male dominance affects men negatively. "One of the striking commonalities throughout much of the literature on men and masculinity is agreement about the cost of being masculine. Even if men themselves are not oppressed, those who assume a traditional masculine role tend to pay a price" (Clatterbaugh, 1990, p. 117).

One price involves emotional expressiveness, intimacy, and interrelatedness, characteristics assigned to the female role and thus stereotypically viewed as belonging exclusively to the female world. Masculine men, "real men," need no one. As I describe later in the chapter, however, male independence is mainly an illusion. Men depend on women to express for them (Pleck, 1981b) and to provide the nurturance that they themselves often are unable to give (Pogrebin, 1983). Another price of the traditional male role is asking men to abdicate their sense of self to the provider role, and hence to an authoritarian system in which they become controlled by the conditions of employment and see other men as their rivals. Real men are successful breadwinners, despite the physical and emotional costs involved.

This chapter first provides a brief history of changes in perceptions of men's roles and masculinity. It then considers struggles these changes pose for individual men, struggles that essentially parallel the two gender dynamics identified for women. What were called dependency and personal achievement when considering the female perspectives are identified as power and the prerogative of male superiority, respectively, when considering the male perspective.

⠧ Men's Changing History

> A man who has been the indisputable favorite of his mother keeps for life the feeling of a conqueror, that confidence of success that often inspires real success. (Freud, "Letters," cited in Sky-Peck, 1991, p. 11)

Women give men strength but never become their rivals. Freud's theory of human development, not unlike those of his forebearers and contemporaries, gave women the power to produce greatness in men but not in themselves. Because of their obvious biological differences, women and men were assumed to have intrinsically different natures, and the social roles and attributes they took on simply reflected their supposedly different essential natures. Thus, men became socially and politically powerful, provided for women and children, and engaged in masculine-affirming activities that often involved danger, risk, sexuality, or competition with other men.

Nonetheless some U.S. men always have embraced feminist principles and advocated for the social, economic, and political equality of women and men (Kimmel, 1989). Henry Blackwell, as noted in the previous chapter, supported women's suffrage and was among the signers of the original Declaration of Sentiments in 1848. Early liberals such as John Stuart Mill (1869/1970) openly defended women's rights: "The moral regeneration of mankind will only really commence, when the most fundamental of the social relations [marriage] is placed under the rule of equal justice, and when human beings learn to cultivate their strongest sympathy with an equal in rights and in cultivation" (p. 95). William Durant, the founder of Wellesley College in 1876, one of the few remaining women's colleges, was an impassioned believer in women's rights. He saw the "real meaning" of higher education for women as freeing them from the slavery in which women were held by the customs of society.

It is noteworthy that given this concern about women, these men were relatively unconcerned with how society and custom restricted men's lives. The effect on men was considered indirect; men lost out because their wives were required to be less than who they were. Some supporters of women's rights, for example, decried the costs to men who lost their sweethearts to the oppressive bonds of traditional femininity. Kimmel (1989) quotes Floyd Dell, a young radical in the 1920s: "It is in the great world that a man finds his sweetheart, and in that narrow little box outside of the world [i.e., marriage] that he loses her" (p. 589).

Liberating women from patriarchy, and not from men, has taken on an important new dimension as we moved from granting women the right to vote in 1920 to granting them economic, social, and political equality today. We have moved from the position that women have rights, as all people do, to the position that women and men have the same rights. Jessie Bernard put her finger on this key difference when she noted that it is easier to push for men's and women's equality in the workplace than to push for equality in the personal lives of women and men. It is easier for a man to want equal justice for women in the world at large than it is for him to embrace in his heart that a woman who is his partner is also his equal—for to do so may require handing over his image of himself as a man (Kahn, 1984).

Ursula Le Guin (1991) provides a perfect example in her review of a biography of Alva Myrdal, written by Sissela Bok: "Gunnar Myrdal was an enlightened man, yet he never accepted his wife's equality. . . . [He] would not allow the pre-eminence of his work to be questioned. Nor would he admit his rivalry with his wife" (p. 13). (Alva, born in 1902, was awarded the Nobel Peace Prize in 1982 and Gunnar, the Nobel Memorial Prize in Economic Science in 1974.) Le Guin, who entitled her book review "Breakout From the Doll's House," details how Alva persisted in her work, and managed the children with help from others, despite the lack of support from what, for the times, was an enlightened husband. Alva engaged in much soul-searching throughout her life and consciously examined her commitment to her family and her own work. Gunnar took for granted his freedom from domestic responsibility and his claim to absolute priority.

Earlier men who defended and welcomed women's rights did not anticipate changes in how they defined themselves as men, and, if anything, resisted changes in male prerogative. To some degree the same is true today. To realize that wisdom, worldly competence, and courage are not solely male attributes is unsettling and disorienting. But to further realize that women do not need men as their benefactors and protectors or that men may depend on women to feel manly cuts to the core of what it means to be a man. As one man married to a highly successful woman in the same field explained:

> I grew up believing I'd inherited a virtual guarantee of special standing. And as an adult things have pretty much gone my way, never forcing me to put my politically correct training to a test [he is an avowed feminist]. So sure, I got the girl, but it seemed unfair that she got me and everything else—prestige, money and public accolades. It's as though her snagging that job was the first of several lessons the universe figured I was owed—lessons about letting go of traditional mantles of power and discovering new and subtle sources of security as a man. (Weiss, 1987, p. 10)

ᐧᕈ Men, Relationships, and Careers

Although the traditional emblems of masculinity abound in the culture at large, many men today question their usefulness and seek new definitions for their self-worth and self-confidence (O'Neil, 1982, in press). Men's greater involvement in relationships, caring, and parenting likely is the hallmark of the 1990s. "I do not know of a way to tell my five-year-old that I don't have time for her, that I have something more important to do," said a man who declined to run for the Senate in 1992, but perhaps will later. Recent surveys show that nearly one third of working fathers have refused a new job, a promotion, or a transfer that threatened to reduce their family time (Malcolm, 1991). Half the men polled by the largest executive recruiting firm in the financial field reported that they would be willing to reduce their hours and salary by up to 25% in order to have more family time (Ball, 1989). Later chapters provide more detail on how changing male perspectives are changing men.

I said earlier that change, societal or personal, rarely comes easily. Such is the case for contemporary men. Some men seem confused about their roles, and still others are trying to redefine masculinity. I now turn to what makes it harder for men to embrace women as their equals rather than as their nurturers and succorers.

Power and the Construction
of Male Independence

Almost nowhere on earth does mere physical maturity make a boy a man (Gilmore, 1990). Manhood is earned or proven through an ideology that glorifies power, toughness, assertiveness, bravery, and independence. Brannon (1985) identified four dimensions of masculinity consistent with this ideology: not being feminine (what Brannon calls "no sissy stuff"); being respected and admired for successful achievement ("the big wheel"); never showing uncertainty or weakness ("the sturdy oak"); and seeking adventure and risk, including the acceptance of violence if necessary ("give 'em hell"). This ideology required men to see themselves as highly independent and self-sufficient and to seek ways of gaining and maintaining power in their world. Education, achievement, sexual prowess, and athletic ability all contributed to men's power.

Power seems particularly crucial to men in our culture—power over women, power over other men, power over sons and daughters. We socialize men to think of themselves as powerful and to feel entitled to those feelings. In reality, most men have little power and find themselves using dominance, authority, and withholding of emotion to construct and maintain images of themselves as powerful men. These constructions take many forms—seeing women as needing them too much, feeling they have sexual access to any woman, feeling entitled to act abusively. Constructions to maintain power inadvertently hurt men by masking their normal dependency, inhibiting their nurturing behaviors and their giving of themselves to strengthen others, and distorting the meaning of their sexual expression.

In relations with women, men's exaggerated independence and need for power becomes manifest as seeing women as longing to care for men. It is a man's prerogative to have women sustain and care for him. After all he is a man. As long as men (and women) conceptualized women's caregiving as something women did for men, neither sex had to acknowledge men's neediness and their dependency on women to feel powerful (recall the dialogue between Mr. and Mrs. Ramsey in the previous chapter). "Sturdy oaks" rely on and need no one but themselves.

Dependency is experienced by all human beings and is a healthy, adaptive, and positive aspect of human development. I have argued elsewhere that female emotional dependency on men was purposely exaggerated to obfuscate men's normal dependency on women, which traditional views of maleness disallowed (Gilbert, 1987b, 1992). The belief that women need men more than men need women not only reinforces men's greater power and independence, but, on a less overt level, also puts men in the position of not being allowed to recognize the depth of their human neediness and thus reinforces their denying their own dependency on women.

What evidence is there for this? For an answer I look to two areas, sexuality and nurturance.

Sexuality is viewed as central to male power. Men must be big where it counts, powerful, and able to take charge successfully. They may also feel a privileged access to or an ownership of women and their bodies. (The spoils of war often included raping the women and girls of the defeated.) Less recognized by men is how they look to women to validate them as men (Pleck, 1981b). Through sexual relations with women, any women, men look for validation of themselves as men. This close association between sexual power and manliness pervades U.S. culture (Brod, 1987).

One power men have over women is sexual power. Only recently have acquaintance rape and sexual harassment exploded into public consciousness. Romantic partners were implicated in 50% to 57% of sexual assaults reported by college-age and adult women (Koss, 1990). I mentioned in the first chapter that only ten years ago sexual harassment was legally unthinkable. Behaviors that we now know constitute sexual harassment were invisible because they characterized "normal" interactions with women in environments where men have more power. Our society allows and condones men making their sexual needs explicit because such needs appear as male rights divorced from emotional neediness. Women are interchangeable objects of men's sexual power, not of men's desperate neediness to feel like a man.

Paradoxically, men both view themselves as more powerful than women and project on women power to make men feel like men. Because men are not supposed to be honestly needful, they also may project their own dependency on women. Many men who see women as wanting too much from them may, in fact, themselves desire a great deal of emotional support and understanding from women. A case in point is a couple in one of our studies. They had been dating for over a year while he had been trying to get out of a marriage with "an extremely dependent wife." This man had fallen in love with an independent career woman who brought him incredible happiness. After much agony and many discussions, he decided he could not leave his wife, regardless of how miserable the marriage, because she needed him too much. He was dependent on her needing him as well as on the sense of power this gave him in his own mind.

Nurturance, in contrast to sexuality, represents the antithesis of male power. Stereotype and tradition said the sexes were opposite, not different. What belonged to one sex could not belong to the other. So nurturing is what women did for men. Women knew how to bring out the best in men be they fictional characters from fairy tales such

Figure 3.1. "And through her nurturance and care, Snow White transformed the seven obscure little men into the world's most famous troupe of singing workers"

as Snow White or wives in the lives of contemporary great men (Figure 3.1).

Brendan Gill (1990) begins his affectionate homage to Lewis Mumford with:

Lewis Mumford died in January, at the age of ninety-four. For most of us, the nineties are enemy country, imprudent to approach and still more imprudent to attain, and Mumford was no exception. For several years, he was both in the world and out of it. Selflessly and heroically, his wife, Sophia, cared for him and protected him, as she had done throughout almost seventy years of marriage, and toward the end there were moments when the light of his mind returned and blazed with much of its old intensity. (p. 90)

Gill goes on to describe Mumford's many noble accomplishments and his great knowledge and vision. Mumford's wife, Sophia, is never again mentioned.

Neil Simon, one of my favorite playwrights, has an affinity for marriage and can't imagine living alone (he is in his third marriage). His first wife, Joan, died of cancer in 1973, and this was a great loss to him. He says of her:

The things I couldn't channel into any other human being—my mother, my father, my brother, anybody—I could channel into Joan, who understood. She was so open, and when I wasn't she'd say, "Why won't you talk? What are you afraid of?" She opened me up, and that's what allowed me to become a playwright. She had an incredible sense of honesty. I couldn't get anything past her. (Richards, 1991, p. 30)

Nurturing the men they love does not come without a cost to women, however. Pogrebin (1983) concluded some years ago that in patriarchal families wives conventionally give the care that husbands take: "Contrary to the popular belief that women have the greater dependency needs, men's [noneconomic] dependency needs are far more insatiable. . . . Sex specialization in caring atrophies men's capacity to give comfort" (p. 197). Still today, marriage benefits men more than women (Thompson & Walker, 1989). As Bernard (1982) notes, it is not the complaints of women that demonstrate how damaging marriage can be for women, but rather the poor mental and emotional health of married women compared to married men or unmarried women. Thus the benefits of female nurturance differ considerably for women and men.

Catherine Bateson (1990) provides a less noble example of male dependency on female nurturance. She describes her experiences as a dean at Amherst College in the 1980s as follows:

I also had not anticipated the extra burdens that went with meeting the expectation of nurturance. The president, for instance, had a wife, several secretaries, and a personal assistant, yet he still demanded a disproportionate amount of caretaking. Although he wouldn't ask me to bring him cups of coffee or perform personal errands, he would ask me to support his morale, cover for him when he was unprepared, prevent his impulsive actions, and listen to him let off steam or think out loud for hours at a time. These were tasks he automatically expected of women, but he also demanded them, to a lesser degree, from the men around him. Yet he appeared to have no sense that he had some caretaking responsibility for his staff, who used to end up in my office, expecting me to nurse them back to self-respect. It took a lot of us to care for the president and keep him in good running order, at the cost of neglecting our other responsibilities. Some of his need was a legitimate balance to the strains of his position; some of it was a habit of being indulged that made me wish parents could rear children without such a core of neediness and without the expectation that others could be used to fill it. (p. 136)

Men like this college president take rather than give care and see it as their due. They fail to see how their insatiable needs require constant attention. From their vantage point, they are high-achieving, successful, independent men—like Mumford and Simon—who have made it to the top.

Another example of male dependency on female nurturance comes from a recent pilot study we conducted on conflict resolution in dual-career marriages. The female spouse, a talented writer and performer, was working half-time in order to develop her own creative work. For the first time in their ten-year marriage, she was earning much less than her spouse. Because she earned so much less they both viewed her as having to take on more of the family work—and take greater care of him. She said: "I feel like I am married to a boy. If I make any requests he pouts or has a temper tantrum. He brings in more of the money and I orchestrate everything else. I most resent his lack of generosity of spirit. He feels entitled to all that I do to keep him propped up." (After several consultations associated with the project, they became clearer on these dynamics and began talking in new ways.)

Assumptions about male power relate to the well-documented gender differences in the patterning of both verbal and nonverbal communication and in topics of discourse (Aries, 1987). Tannen (1990) argues that women and men fail to understand one another because men see themselves in a hierarchical social order in which they are either one-up or one-down. In the world as they construe it, conversations are negotiations in which people try either to achieve the upper hand or protect themselves from others' attempts to have the upper hand and put them down. Women, in contrast, she argues, perceive themselves as part of a network of connections. In the world as they know it, conversations are negotiations for closeness in which people try to "seek and give confirmation and support, and to reach consensus" (p. 25).

Men's difficulty in establishing close working relations with women may relate to men's self-view that they should control and dominate interactions with women (McGill, 1985; Pleck, 1981b). Withholding themselves from relations with women not only provides men with the illusion of an independent stance but also reinforces their dominant position. But, as Pleck (1981b) also points out, by engaging in these kinds of interactions, men give women the ability to make them feel like men, because maintaining their dominant position depends on women seeing men as superior to them.

The Prerogative of Male Superiority

A New York Times telephone poll conducted in 1989 indicated that 77% of male respondents aged 18 to 44 agreed with the statement, "Men's attitudes toward women have changed for the better in the past 20 years"; however, 53% also agreed with the statement, "Most men they know think they are better than women" (Belkin, 1989). White men in our culture characteristically grow up with feelings of confidence and specialness granted them simply because they are born male. This specialness becomes an essential aspect of male entitlement, which encourages men to feel that what they do or want takes precedence over the needs of women and that their prerogatives should not be questioned. Men may view even small losses of advantage or deference as large threats (Goode, 1982) because their sense of self is so closely tied to their entitlement, especially in relation to women. Men's assumed superiority still is quite prevalent among women and men. I have argued elsewhere that as a result, many men today likely grow up with feelings of confidence and specialness granted them simply because they are born male (cf. Gilbert, 1987a, 1992). This specialness is an essential aspect of male entitlement, which encourages men (and women) to feel that what men do or want should take precedence over the needs of women and that men's prerogatives should not be questioned. A man in one study (Gilbert, 1988) said: "I've heard complaints from many single women that they can't trust any man's willingness to support their careers. Men they date say they love independence in a woman, but they don't waste a second demolishing it brick by brick. Many men I speak to think women are right" (p. 64).

Among spouses in dual-career families this entitlement becomes evident in such ways as more locations and relocations occurring for the male spouse than the female spouse, and in marriage benefitting men more than women because men are entitled to nurturance, higher salaries, more opportunities for advancement, and less family work (Barnett & Baruch, 1987b; Gilbert, 1988).

Two aspects of men's assumed superiority often emerge in relationships with women. The first is not recognizing women's needs for independence. The second is an exaggerated sense of self-importance.

Simmons (1988) provides an interesting illustration of a woman's need for independence in describing his mother's largely unsuccessful struggles for self-definition in her marriage to a very traditional man. She married in the 1950s and over time "in a confused way . . . knew that all the pleasant clichés she had learned about love and marriage and child rearing had deceived her intolerably" (p. 9). What stands out for him now are her "small rebellions," most notably her trip alone to Europe in 1967, paid for with her own money by working two temporary jobs against her husband's wishes.

Rather than seeing women's small or large rebellions as a legitimate need for independence, male partners, like this woman's husband, often devalue women by accusing female partners of dishonorable motivations, or by using patronizing tones. A case in point is a young professional woman who felt too dependent on her boyfriend of seven years and wanted to live on her own for a while and not see him on a regular basis. She carefully and lovingly explained to him how she needed to feel strong in herself before entering into a marriage with him. He could not understand. His immediate response was, "Do it if you want, but that's the end of our relationship." Later in the conversation he referred to her as wanting to whore around, a motivation that made sense from his perspective, but that showed a profound lack of understanding of his partner. A woman wanting and needing to be strong in herself simply did not compute for this man. It just was not necessary. Likely, it also was very threatening for him to even consciously consider. Having women dependent on them keeps men from viewing female partners as their equals.

Men's exaggerated sense of self-importance makes it harder for men to listen to women and to consider women's requests as legitimate or having merit. The world is seen from their perspective. I recall a slide I showed when I first lectured to audiences on the topic of dual-career families. Two men are standing in the kitchen conversing and enjoying a glass of wine while their female partners are preparing dinner. One of them says to the women, "John and I have decided that we are sick of hearing about women and their problems" (Koren, 1979).

Findings from a recent study (Weiss, 1991) of upper middle-class, heterosexual, white men who do well at work remind me of this earlier slide. Although most female spouses were employed, the 70 men in the survey showed little concern with their wives' lives or with how they managed to juggle work and family. "Being a good man means being able to maintain a respected place among men, being able to serve as head to a family and as a model to one's children" (p. 229). Weiss sees no reason that men who are doing reasonably well, "good men," need to or should change the underlying structure of their lives as entitled men. Why create marital conflict and divisiveness?

Another male author provides an insightful response (Chassler, 1984):

> The next night *I* decided to do the dishes and *she* read the paper. [There had been some tension about this the night before.] At the sink, I began to think about male arrogance. Why did I have the choice of doing or not doing the dishes, while my wife did not? By the same token, why had she had to wait until our children were in school to exercise her "free" choice of working at her career? Our jobs were equally pressured and difficult (hers more harrowing than mine) and yet, if I chose to sit and read after dinner, I could. She could not, unless I decided she could by *offering* to do the dishes. My definition of freedom was based on a white male conception: the notion that because I am free, because I can make choices, anyone can make choices. I was defining "anyone" in my terms as a man. (p. 52)

An exaggerated sense of self-importance can keep men from seeing the reality of women's lives and from supporting changes that would benefit women. Rather than pitching in to cook dinner or clean up, they wait to be asked. Their time is too important to devote to "women's work." One man I know, who lived with a female partner, took her out to dinner whenever she complained that he was not doing his fair share of the meal preparation. He saw this as "fair"; she saw it as his "not getting it" and eventually left the relationship. Rather than considering alterations to their own lives, some men view having a child as a woman's choice: If she wants a child badly enough, she will have to do what's necessary; my life is too important.

These are extreme views, yet they remain unspoken in many men's minds. It is very hard to give up an exaggerated sense of self-importance vis-à-vis women, when doing so is viewed as part of the male prerogative.

❧ Summary

This chapter and the previous one inform one another. Chapter 2 discussed vestiges of traditional female socialization that centered around what makes women desirable to men. Still today, we learned, women must counter and grapple with internalized and societal notions of male superiority, privilege, and power. This chapter considered the social constructions of male power and prerogative central to masculinity and illustrated how these factors become manifest in interpersonal processes between women and men and between men. Many men, for instance, may feel entitled to having women serve their needs at home or work or having women support their goals without having to earn or request it. Financially providing for a partner or a date may become automatically associated with special privilege, sexual or otherwise. I recall the one piece of advice I gave my 18-year-old daughter when she went off to college: "Always pay your own way."

These dynamics, unflattering and destructive as they may be at times, have their roots in traditional notions of what it means to be a man. Men today are moving beyond traditional gendered definitions of themselves, but giving up familiar sources of power and self-definition does not come easily. The next two chapters explore these gender issues within the context of unmarried and married women and men. First I consider the intentions and expectations of single young adults regarding future partners and future life goals, and then I turn to the day-to-day realities of partners in dual-career families.

.

TWO

Expectations for and Realities of Dual-Career Family Life

4

❧

Young Adults' Career and Family Intentions and Expectations

Changing sex-specialized norms and sex-typed behavior is not a
take-it-or-leave-it option. It is a fundamental imperative. The question is not whether to do it, but rather how to do it. (Bernard, 1976,
p. 222)

Nearly all women and men planning careers assume they will
be in long-term romantic relationships (Spade & Reese, 1991;
Tittle, 1981). Yet little historical precedent exists for relationships in
which both partners involve themselves in continuous careers and
family life. This chapter uses my research and the work of others to
address such questions as: (a) What do young heterosexual adults preparing themselves for careers today expect in the way of marriage
and child-rearing? (b) What characteristics do they desire in partners?
(c) How do they envision their life and what possible difficulties and
conflicts do they anticipate?

Earlier chapters described how gender processes interface career
development and romantic relationships. Preferences for romantic
partners and careers reflect individuals' uniqueness, their gender
socialization, and the times. In the past women's economic dependence on men became associated with a preference for male partners

who would be good providers. Men, in turn, preferred women who enhanced their image and success as men.

Most women today provide for themselves economically. Career-minded heterosexual women typically want partners who see women as their equals, not their nurturers, and who do their fair share in making a dual-career relationship work. Pervasive gender-related dynamics, if not recognized, may inhibit or undermine egalitarian intentions, however. Of particular concern would be discrepancies between the priority and planning young women give to integrating work and family, compared to such planning by men. This situation, which essentially perpetuates things as they are, would work against gender equality and the notion of role-sharing marriages. Women, regardless of their interests and abilities, would be allowed "role expansion." This means they would maintain their traditional home roles and also engage in occupational work. Men, regardless of their talents and interests, would help out at home and hold their careers as primary. No changes would be needed in workplace policies or in the structure of occupational work. Such discrepancies would be embedded in and maintained by the gender processes described in the first chapter. Views of men as entitled and superior and women as nurturers and enablers would further perpetuate these conditions and circumstances.

ɞ The Situation Today

> I'm afraid if I fall in love I will lose my competitive edge. (unsolicited comment from Gilbert, Dancer, Rossman, & Thorn, 1991 study)

Women and men contemplating dual-career marriages still face somewhat different realities. Women more than men push for partnerships, and when push comes to shove, women accommodate to men's careers more than men accommodate to women's careers (Thompson & Walker, 1989). Most heterosexual men who have access to educational opportunities assume they will enter careers, marry, and have children. Little thought is given to conflicts between paid work and family life or to how marriage and children will influence chosen career paths. In contrast, most women give considerable thought to how careers will be integrated with long-term relationships and children.

Studies indicate that high school girls more than boys think ahead to what families would mean for their occupational aspirations. Tittle (1981), for example, studied middle-class, urban 11th-graders. Most expected to work full-time after completing their formal education, but women, not men, assumed they would interrupt or modify work schedules for children. A later study of middle-class adolescents from grades 6, 8, 10, and 12 reported that girls and boys both desired careers; girls alone saw dilemmas ahead, however (Archer, 1985). Girls assumed husbands would not involve themselves in family work and they themselves would receive little support for integrating work and family roles. Farmer (1985) studied the same age group as Archer, but used a much larger sample of 9th- and 12th-graders and included measures of perceived support. Three aspects of environmental support were assessed: parents' support for students' school achievement, teachers' support for their career plans, and anticipated support for working women/men from future spouses and employers. As was hypothesized, the mediating effect of environmental support on motivational dimensions (aspirations, mastery, and career commitment) was stronger for young women than for young men in the study. That is, current support for career goals from parents and teachers and assumed support from future spouses and employers were more strongly associated with the aspirations and career commitment of girls than with those of boys. These findings indicate that regardless of the kind of support they receive from significant others, boys know they are expected to achieve occupationally. Girls, however, appear more sensitive to support from significant others for their career aspirations and career commitment.

Studies with college-aged, lower-division, predominantly white undergraduate populations report similar findings. Ganong and Coleman (1992) asked students to respond to single-item scales about professional success. Male and female students reported comparable estimates of their desire for, and potential to, achieve personal success and educational goals. When asked to compare themselves to a future spouse, however, female respondents thought their marital partner should be more professionally successful than themselves, and male respondents thought future wives should be less success-ful. Spade and Reese (1991) reported a similar kind of inconsistency. Both female and male students in their study expected occupational work to be central in their lives, but only 47% of male respondents, compared to 89% of female respondents, preferred that their spouse be employed if the respondent made enough money to support the family.

ʒ۰ My Studies of Young Adults

Erikson (1968) described young adults as striving to achieve a self-definition that not only gives them a sense of knowing where they are going but that also is met with support and approval from the significant others in their lives, particularly parents and other influential adults. According to Erikson, attaining a sense of inner identity represents the ability of individuals to adapt their special skills, capacities, and strengths to the prevailing role structure of society. In the past this meant that women and men lived separate lives. The emergence of the dual-earner family as the modal family form, within the larger context of women's increased opportunities and status, represents a changing role structure. Individuals today, regardless of sex, must consider their life choices within the broader framework of combining work and family rather than of precluding one or the other. The traditional framework of conceptual dichotomies—career versus parenthood, his career versus her career—no longer predicts how individuals will live their adult lives. Instead, adults today face the challenge of considering how these formerly differentiated roles can be integrated and combined. Yet the literature indicates that women more than men are grappling with the issues of integration and combination.

My research interest was in going beyond the general gender differences reported in studies of middle-class high school and lower-division college populations to young adults who were closer to entering careers. Furthermore, among young adults there are differences in future planning; not all women and men aspire to or actually enter into careers or dual-career relationships. People vary in their abilities, their ambitions, their attitudes, their passions, and their life experiences. If we looked at young women and men who were close to completing their college degrees, would we still find that women, but not men, planned to combine work and family?

Pursuing this interest in young adults required that we first develop instruments that would allow us to identify college-aged women and men who envisioned themselves as partners in dual-career families. Once we had developed the measures, we were in a position to look more specifically at young adults who envision a role-sharing, dual-career family life. Do they differ from their peers on such gender-related variables as attitudes toward women's and men's roles and needs for male superiority? Do certain environmental or family factors enhance or inhibit the emergence of possible selves that integrate work and family?

The next section first describes the instruments we developed to investigate gender-related aspects of dual-career family life. I then summarize findings from a series of studies with university juniors and seniors. Consistent with Babitz's (1979) view that "It's the frames from which the content arises," key variables in the studies were the family context in which individuals grew up and their mothers' and fathers' behaviors with regard to family work and careers.

Gender-Related Measures
Developed to Study Perceptions
of Work and Family in Young Adults

The first step in the research was developing measures that fit the times. The literature available indicated variations among dual-earner families, and we needed a way to identify individuals interested in the kind of role-sharing dual-career relationships envisioned by the Rapoports (1969) (for descriptions of these variations, see Chapter 5). The *Orientations to Occupational-Family Integration Scale*, or OOFI, was developed to respond to this need (Gilbert, Dancer, Rossman, & Thorn, 1991).

Certain gender processes compromise egalitarian goals. Earlier chapters discussed the concepts of dependency, personal achievement, and the prerogative of male superiority. The *Essential Characteristics of Spouse Scales* were developed to assess current percep- tions of these gender-related concepts, particularly as they relate to desired life partners (Gilbert et al., 1991).

Finally, well-meaning young women and men naively aspire to and/or enter dual-career family life without understanding obstacles and realities associated with gender. These, too, were discussed in earlier chapters. Catalyst (1987), for example, an organization concerned with women's career development, explored the attitudes about work and family among college students at six diverse campuses (for a description of the organization, see Chapter 1). A main conclusion of the study was that students wanted satisfying careers and meaningful personal lives, but they had a limited understanding of the realities involved, such as salary expectations, parental leave policies, and difficulties typically experienced by working parents. The *Future Difficulties Scales* were developed to assess young adults' perceptions in these areas (Gilbert et al., 1991).

Most women and men today grow up with the assumption that they will be employed. How that employment fits with family roles varies. The *Orientations to Occupational-Family Integration* (OOFI) Scale describes three orientations: male traditional/conventional, female traditional/conventional, and male and female atraditional or role-sharing. Items on the female and male traditional/conventional scales reflect the view that although women and men may both be employed, the woman holds primary responsibility for the home and children and the man holds primary responsibility for providing economically. In contrast, items on the role-sharing scale reflect the active integration of occupational and family roles for the person responding and for that person's partner. Endorsement of these items represents an ongoing thoughtful consideration of and commitment to engaging in both occupational and family work.

The items on the three scales of the OOFI, together with ten filler items (e.g., I see myself married someday; I see myself working full-time after I finish my formal education) are presented as a single instrument in which the order of the items is randomized. Respondents are instructed: "Currently our society is experiencing changes. As a result of these changes there are many different possibilities for handling work and family roles as an adult. We'd like to know how much you have thought about each possibility, at this time in your life, and how much you see yourself committed to choosing this possibility for yourself." Using 5-point Likert scales that range from "not at all" (1) to "very much" (5), respondents first indicate how much they have thought about or considered the option described in each item, and then indicate the degree to which they feel committed to the option at the present time. Although respondents are asked to complete all the OOFI items, only women receive scores on the female traditional/conventional scale and males on the male traditional/conventional scale. Sample items are as follows (also see Table 4.1).

OOFI Female Traditional/Conventional Scale (OOFI-F-T/C):
- After marriage I see my spouse as being the major financial provider and working full-time.
- After marriage I see myself working part-time and taking primary responsibility for raising the children.

OOFI Male Traditional/Conventional Scale (OOFI-M-T/C):
- I see my spouse pretty much taking responsibility for raising the children.
- I see my spouse's income as providing extra money.

OOFI Role-Sharing Scale (OOFI-RS):
- I see my spouse and I both working full-time and sharing the financial responsibility continuously throughout our marriage.
- With or without children I see myself and my spouse to a great extent sharing the day-to-day responsibilities for maintaining the household, like food shopping, cooking, laundry, and routine money management.

The *Essential Characteristics of Spouse Scales* consist of three scales, Career Success Traits, Emotional/Relational Traits, and Views of Family Life. Essentially the scales describe characteristics associated with traditional and changing views of what is desirable and attractive in the women and men we would want for partners.

The instructions for responding to the scales read: "We just asked you about ways you plan or do not plan to combine work and family with a spouse. Now we would like to know what you want in a future partner. What are the qualities that you view as important in that person?" Responses are made on 5-point Likert scales that range from "not at all essential" (1 on the scale) to "very essential" (5). Illustrative items appear below and in Table 4.2.

Career Success Traits
- Someone who pursues their own interests and goals
- Someone who is able to be independent financially
- Someone who is strong and confident

Emotional/Relational Traits
- Someone who makes me feel needed
- Someone who puts me first
- Someone who is warm and nurturing

Views of Family Life
- Someone who shares daily household tasks
- Someone who will alter her/his work schedule for parenting
- Someone who holds traditional views of men's roles (reverse scored)

Finally, the *Future Difficulties Scales* consist of three scales: Child Care, Spouses Sharing Family Work, and Career Advancement. (The next chapter describes these difficulties in some detail.) In responding to the scales, young adults are told: "We have asked you a number of questions about how you envision your future life and what you prefer or wish. Now we would like to know what you see as possible barriers or difficulties to achieving the kind of life you now envision for yourself." Each difficulty is rated on a 5-point Likert scale that ranges from "not at all an anticipated difficulty" (1) to "very much an anticipated difficulty" (5). Representative items on the scales are as follows:

Child Care
- Finding good child care
- Using child care for a preschool-aged child

Spouses Sharing Family Work
- Getting my spouse to really share household work
- Getting my spouse to really share parenting

Career Advancement
- Feeling a lot of conflict if I continue my career and have a child
- Having the freedom to locate or relocate professionally
- Having to work more than I want to

Readers interested in how they would score on these scales are referred to Tables 4.1 and 4.2. Other measures used in the studies are mentioned in describing the findings (e.g., self-esteem, parents' involvement in work and family).

Research Questions and Major Findings

In all we have conducted a series of four studies. For reasons that become clear later, participants in the study were from families in which parents were still married to one another. Initial studies focused on correlates of the OOFI scales (Gilbert et al., 1991). Later studies addressed specific hypotheses about environmental or family factors influencing the emergence of possible selves that integrate occupational career and family (Gilbert & Dancer, 1992; Gilbert, Rossman, & Thorn, 1991; Gilbert, Rossman, Hallett, & Habib, 1992).

Question #1:
What relevant variables correlate
with scores on the OOFI Role-Sharing
and Traditional/Conventional Scales?

University juniors and seniors "who definitely viewed themselves as getting into a long-term relationship with someone of the other (opposite) sex" completed the measures just described, together with measures of self-esteem, attitudes (how liberal participants considered themselves with regard to views of work and family), and commitment to employment in adulthood. Only respondents who indicated that their parents were still married were included in the data analyses. As anticipated, women scoring higher on the OOFI-RS Thought and Commitment scales, and thus having a higher commitment to achieving a role-sharing marriage, reported more liberal attitudes, had a higher commitment to employment throughout adulthood, ascribed higher importance to spouse characteristics that reflect a sharing of home roles, and anticipated less difficulty in using child care and advancing in their careers.

A somewhat different pattern emerged for men on the OOFI-RS scale. Men scoring higher on the OOFI-RS scale ascribed higher importance to spouse characteristics that reflect a sharing of home roles and to spouse characteristics associated with career success and economic independence. Higher scorers also anticipated more difficulty advancing in their careers.

Table 4.1 How Would You Describe Yourself?

	How Much You've Thought 1 2 3 4 5		How Much You're Committed 1 2 3 4 5	
	Not at all	Very much	Not at all	Very much

After marriage (before or with children):

1. I see my spouse and I both working full-time and sharing the financial responsibility continuously throughout our marriage.

2. I see myself and my spouse both employed full-time and to a great extent sharing the day to day responsibilities for maintaining the household, like food shopping, cooking, laundry, and routine money management.

3. I see myself working full-time and being the major financial provider.

4. I see myself preferring not to work and will work only for additional income.

5. I see my spouse as working full-time and being the major financial provider.

6. I see my spouse working only for additional income.

7. I see myself working part-time and taking primary responsibility for maintaining the household.

8. I see my spouse as working part- or full-time and taking primary responsibility for both maintaining the household and raising the children.

9. I see myself and my spouse both employed part-time and to a great extent sharing the day to day responsibilities for both maintaining the household and raising the children.

10. I see myself working full-time and taking primary responsibility for raising the children.

NOTE: The complete scales are not reproduced here. Key: OOFI-F-T/C (4, 5, 7, 10); OOFI-M-T/C (3, 6, 8); OOFI-RS (1, 2, 9).

The different correlational patterns for women and men reflect their different realities. Women and men contemplating role-sharing

Table 4.2 How Would You Describe Yourself?

We have just asked you about ways to combine work and family with a future spouse. Now we would like to know what you want in a future partner. What are the qualities that you now view as important in that person? Listed below are a number of characteristics. Please indicate the degree of importance of each characteristic by using a scale that ranges from not at all important (1) to essential (5).

	Not at all important 1 2 3 4 5 *Essential*
1. Someone who shares my spiritual values	1 2 3 4 5
2. Someone who is attractive to me	1 2 3 4 5
3. Someone who shares my viewpoints and interests	1 2 3 4 5
4. Someone who will alter his/her work schedule for parenting	1 2 3 4 5
5. Someone who pursues his or her own interests and goals	1 2 3 4 5
6. Someone who makes me feel needed	1 2 3 4 5
7. Someone who is warm and nurturing	1 2 3 4 5
8. Someone who makes me feel protected and secure	1 2 3 4 5
9. Someone who is strong and self-confident	1 2 3 4 5
10. Someone who is considerate and listens to me	1 2 3 4 5
11. Someone who is able to be independent financially	1 2 3 4 5
12. Someone who will be supportive of my career	1 2 3 4 5
13. Someone who shares daily household tasks (e.g., cooking)	1 2 3 4 5
14. Someone who holds traditional views of men's roles*	1 2 3 4 5
15. Someone who will be successful in his or her career	1 2 3 4 5
16. Someone who shares the daily tasks of child rearing (e.g., diapering)	1 2 3 4 5

NOTE: The complete scales are not reproduced here. Key to Essential Characteristics of Spouse Scales: filler items (1, 2, 3), career success traits (5, 9, 11, 15), emotional/relational traits (6, 7, 8, 10, 12), views of family life (4, 13, 14, 16).
* = Reverse-scored item

marriages both want spouses who share daily household tasks and alter work schedules for parenting. But college-educated women assume future spouses will be high on career success traits regardless of their commitment to role-sharing relationships. This scale has little variability for female respondents: Career success traits are still essential characteristics in a husband today. A "Cathy" cartoon strip provides a humorous but poignant example (Guisewite, 1988). Cathy first tells Irving, her boyfriend, that what women want from men is to be treated with integrity and with honest respect for her as a human being. She goes on to say, "Also, you have to look like that [a male actor on TV] and make $300,000 a year."

College-educated men, in contrast, vary more when it comes to career success traits in a wife. Men who saw themselves as more committed to role-sharing relationships viewed career success traits in their future spouse as more important. With regard to future difficulties, a higher commitment to role sharing was associated with less anticipated difficulty advancing in their careers, for women, but more anticipated difficulty for men. These findings definitely fit the data for actual couples. Role-sharing generally benefits women's careers but places some constraints on men's careers (Gilbert, 1985). Finally, scores on attitudes and views of employment were associated with scores on the OOFI-RS scales for women but not for men. In contrast to the women in the sample, the young men assumed a commitment to employment regardless of involvement in other life roles.

Correlational patterns for the OOFI-T/C scales were very much as expected. Women scoring higher on the OOFI-T/C scales reported more traditional attitudes and lower commitment to employment and ascribed less importance to spouse characteristics that reflect a sharing of home roles. Men scoring higher on the OOFI-T/C scales reported more traditional attitudes and higher commitment to employment throughout the life cycle. With regard to their future spouse, as would be expected, men expressing a higher commitment to traditional roles rated as less essential spouse characteristics that reflect career success traits and sharing of home roles, and as more essential characteristics associated with being nurtured and taken care of. (In this and later studies self-esteem was not related to OOFI responses.)

In conclusion, scores on the OOFI-RS Scales and OOFI-T/C Scales correlate with other measures in expected ways. Female and male college-educated young adults more committed to role-sharing marriages desired future spouses whose personal characteristics more reflected a sharing of home roles and, for males, more reflected career success traits. With regard to future difficulties, women more committed to role-sharing marriages anticipated less difficulty with child care and career advancement, and men more difficulty with career advancement.

Question #2:
What contextual family variables
influence young adults' expectations
and intentions about work and family?

Both female and male children of employed mothers hold less stereotypic attitudes about gender roles than do children of nonemployed mothers. Early studies attributed these findings to the effect of maternal employment itself. Later studies have broadened explanations to include variables influenced by women's employment. For example, women's greater economic independence and increased opportunity in the society at large influence children's images of what women can do and become.

My interest was in a second variable influenced by women's employment—men's involvement in family work (Barnett & Baruch, 1987b; Hoffman, 1989). Two aspects of men's behaviors in the home appear particularly crucial to children's developing self-concepts—role modeling and motivations for involvement in home and family roles. Male partners in dual-earner families, like female partners, may model less stereotypic behaviors, behaviors that provide children with alternative images of male and female attributes and role-related behaviors. For instance, in our studies of men in dual-career families, fathers whom raters judged to be more involved in parenting rated themselves as closer to their children and rated being a parent and having a sense of family as more important than did those judged to be less involved (Gilbert, 1985).

Also important may be fathers' actual involvement in family work, the motivations for this involvement, and the effects of these kinds of experiences. Participation in child-rearing and household work by fathers in single-earner, two-parent families as well as in dual-earner families likely is motivated by individual preferences and motivations quite independent of changes in gender-role preferences and behaviors. Self-comfort and perceived competence as a parent, for instance, increase men's participation (Crouter, Perry-Jenkins, Huston, & McHale, 1987). Husbands may enjoy cooking or involvement in child-rearing. A number of fathers in our studies wanted a closeness with their children that they never had with their own father, or they "simply loved children" (Gilbert, 1985, 1988). In fact, both in traditional single-earner, two-parent families and in dual-earner families fathers spend more time with children than in the past (Pleck, 1987). But overall, men today involve themselves more with parenting than with household work (e.g., Gilbert, 1985; Pleck, 1985).

In dual-earner families, however, men's motivations for participating in family work also have to do with the marital and family situation itself. Regardless of, or in addition to, personal preferences and motivations, the realities of two working parents place demands on husbands to engage in household work and parenting activities. Employed wives typically push for husbands' increased participation, particularly if wives prefer to be employed (Thompson & Walker, 1989). Studies indicate several variations of men's participation in dual-earner families that range from traditional/conventional to role-sharing. In traditional/conventional dual-earner families, both spouses are employed, but the wife takes major responsibility for household work and parenting. In essence, the wife moves into the "role expansion" mentioned earlier, and the husband's role changes very little. Role-sharing dual-career families, in contrast, fit the description envisioned by the Rapoports (1969) in that both spouses involve themselves in occupational and family work. (Chapter 5 describes these variations in greater detail.)

Husbands' dissimilar motivations and behaviors among the various single-earner and dual-earner patterns provide different family environments for children and communicate different gendered realities, which children then assimilate into their developing self-schemas. For example, in contrast to the traditional family situation in which the employment role is taken on by the husband and the home roles by the wife, men's family participation in dual-earner situations, particularly role-sharing dual-earner families, reflects a merging of spouses' roles.

Our approach to investigating men's involvement in family work focused on two structural variables related to women's employment: family context and the male partner's involvement in family work. In our studies, family context refers to the kind of two-parent intact family in which young adults were reared. Of most interest were comparisons between traditional male single-earner families and two kinds of dual-earner families—dual-career families and dual-worker families in which both spouses did not describe themselves as pursuing careers. Involvement in family work refers to men's reported participation in household work and in parenting.

Data were again gathered from university juniors and seniors who envisioned a long-term heterosexual relationship and whose parents were still married to each other. In addition to the instruments already described, respondents completed questions about their parents' educational and occupational lives and their parents' satisfaction with their employment and marriage, and indicated each parent's overall level of participation in a number of household and parenting activities while respondents were growing up. Responses were made on a 5-point Likert scale that ranged from "not at all involved" (1) to "very involved" (5). Scale scores for household work and parenting were obtained by adding responses to the items in the respective area of family work.

We anticipated that sons and daughters reared in dual-career environments, as compared to peers reared in the other family types studied, were the most likely to develop self-views reflecting the integrating of occupational and family work and would view their fathers as most participating in household work. Across family types, we predicted that children who perceived their father as more involved in household work would report higher scores on both the OOFI-RS scale and the Spouse Characteristics scale, scales reflecting a sharing of home roles, and lower scores on the OOFI-T/C scale and the Future Difficulties scale. Similar predictions were not made for involvement in parenting because of evidence for men's overall increased participation in parenting in middle-class, intact, white families (Dancer & Gilbert, in press; Pleck, 1987).

Our results were very much as predicted. In all three studies, family context was found to be related to responses on the OOFI and to responses on career-related and parent-related variables as well. Of the three family types, young women and men reared in dual-career families reported the highest commitment to role-sharing in marriage, saw their fathers as most participating in daily household chores, and reported the least anticipated difficulty in spouses' sharing home responsibilities and the lowest commitment to marriages in which women and men both worked but women assumed major responsibility for the household and children. Parallel to the first study, males reared in dual-career families anticipated more difficulty advancing in their careers than did females. Also, compared to male peers reared in dual-earner and traditional families, male participants reared in dual-career families reported themselves to be more expressive on the Personal Attributes Questionnaire and to rate career success characteristics as more essential in a future partner.

Finally, plausible differences occurred between female respondents whose mothers were in jobs versus careers. Young women whose mothers held jobs rated future difficulties for themselves more likely, particularly in the areas of their own career advancement and their future spouse sharing household work. Also, young women whose mothers were in careers saw both their mothers and their fathers as more satisfied and as having higher marital satisfaction. These response patterns likely reflect veridical observations of their own parents' behavior. Greater overload typically is experienced by wives when occupational and family roles are not appreciably redefined between spouses. If husbands' occupational work is assumed to be primary in that they have the career and their spouses have a job or a less important career, and/or if husbands (and wives) feel some ambivalence about wives' employment, roles remain less redefined and more traditional.

Conclusions From the Research

I now turn to the three questions initially posed and use data from our studies and those of other researchers to provide informed responses. The first question was, "What do young adults who prepare themselves for careers expect in the way of marriage and child-rearing?" Nearly all these young adults expect to be in long-term relationships and to rear children. Respondents in our studies, for example, were asked how much they had thought about and how committed they were to being married someday, working full-time after they finished their formal schooling, and being a parent someday. On a 5-point scale that ranged from "not at all" (1) to "very much" (5), the means for both women and men were all above 4.5. In the large undergraduate sample studied by Spade and Reese (1991), 99% of women and men agreed that having a good marriage and a family was important to them. Women and men also were similar in their commitment to paid work: 94% of male respondents and 93% of female respondents expected that work would be central to their adult lives. Findings from other studies support those reported here (e.g., Tittle, 1981).

Although on average both women and men in our studies saw themselves moderately committed to role-sharing marriages, women's mean scores were higher than men's in all four studies. The difference between male and female scores was least for respondents reared in dual-career families and most for those reared in traditional male single-earner families, again indicating the importance of family context to self-views. Similarly, on average men reported more commitment to marriages in which they were the primary breadwinner (i.e., higher scores on the OOFI-T/C scale) than did women. Here again, this was most true for respondents reared in male single-earner families and least true for those reared in dual-career families.

The second question was, "What characteristics do young adults desire in partners and why?" Of those available, our studies most explicitly look at future spouse characteristics. Generally speaking young women and men want future partners to be high on characteristics we assigned to the Relational/Emotional and Career/Success Scales. At the same time, regardless of their family context growing up, women, more than men, give greater importance to these spouse characteristics, particularly career success traits in future spouses. The findings of Ganong and Coleman (1992) reflected similar views. On average female college students in their study expected husbands to be more successful than themselves.

These conclusions need to be modified by other variables, however. Women and men more committed to role-sharing in marriage give greater importance to spouse characteristics that reflect participation in family work; men more committed to role-sharing relationships give more importance to career success traits in a future spouse. Family context also appears important. Participants reared in dual-career family environments place more importance on emotional-relational and home participation traits in future spouses than do their peers reared in dual-wage and traditional male single-earner families.

The third question was, "How do young adults envision their life and what conflicts do they see ahead?" Several studies in addition to our own indicate that young adults have some awareness of inevitable conflicts ahead for those envisioning dual-career family life (e.g., Covin & Brush, 1991; Spade & Reese, 1991). Career-oriented college students know about potential difficulties in such areas as child care, spouses really sharing home roles, and career advancement. They also have some awareness that sex-role stereotypes still operate in the workplace and that family-responsive employer policies are essential for employed spouses (Covin & Brush, 1991). Overall though, the mean scores on scales assessing potentially difficult areas hovered around scale midpoints (responses were made on 5-point scales that ranged from "not at all a difficulty for me" [1] to "very much a difficulty for me" [5]). The midrange ratings may indicate that respondents feel sufficiently prepared for possible conflicts and thus see them as posing only modest difficulties. Or they may reflect respondents' underestimating potential difficulties because the areas they were asked to consider were not yet a part of their life experiences.

Here again, other variables help in interpreting responses. Young women and men reared in dual-career family environments anticipated fewer future difficulties. Also, participants who rated their fathers as more involved in household work anticipated less difficulty in spouses sharing family work. Thus respondents who had greater familiarity with ways to combine work and family anticipated fewer future difficulties in the areas assessed.

We can conclude that young adults who grow up in families in which the integration of occupational and family roles is modeled, and probably encouraged, are more likely to develop a sense of self that reflects these experiences. Women and men appear to be similarly influenced. At the same time, regardless of family context and father involvement, women more than men give greater importance to career success traits in future spouses and see more difficulties ahead in areas of child care and family life. Thus, although growing numbers of women and men assume they will combine paid work and family life and seek relationships in which this is possible, men appear less likely to consider how their spouse's employment and the realities of children will affect their plans.

ᴥ Words of Advice for Career-Oriented Young Adults

And will you take my name even if you wind up making more money than I do? (Hamilton, 1987, p. 140)

Young women and men have more choices about love and work than ever before. Many thoughts go through their heads on any given day, as the two illustrations of the average female and average male of the early feminist era, circa 1993, indicate (Figures 4.1, p. 76, and 4.2, p. 77). Some thoughts are quite parallel, whereas others are quite different. Many thoughts reflect their gendered realities.

In the past educated heterosexual women planned their futures around marriage and concerned themselves with paid work only if their husbands needed them to or if they never married. For men, occupational work was a given and formed the fabric of their lives. Over the past few decades, this situation has changed dramatically. Most women and men today plan to be employed, and many assume they will hold positions in professional fields. What planning can these young adults do to better prepare for their adult lives?

Planning ahead means thinking about expectations for yourself and a future spouse and communicating these early on in serious relationships. Different patterns of combining occupations and family life are possible, and partners need to think through which pattern best fits their needs and goals. Gilbert (1985) found that heterosexual partners who achieved role-sharing marriages discussed during courtship what their expectations were for themselves and their future partner in areas such as career pursuits, caring for children, and managing household work. Those who did not discuss such issues in advance were more likely to find themselves in traditional patterns that they had neither wanted nor anticipated. Areas of dual-career family life that need to be discussed with potential partners include the importance of having a partner who can be financially independent, can contribute to the family income, can be successful in a career, etc.; attitudes about women and men, particularly

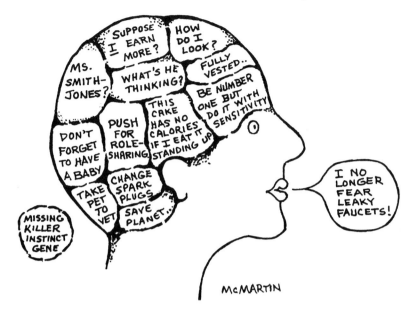

Figure 4.1. Thoughts of Average Female of Early Feminist Era, Circa 1993

whether men are viewed as entitled and superior; the importance of family life, relationships with children, and involvement in child-rearing as reflected, for example, in the willingness to alter one's own work schedule or career path for parenting responsibilities; and so on. Clearly a man who believes that women should not work outside the home or a woman or man who devalues the abilities and goals of her or his partner would not be a good candidate for a role-sharing, dual-career relationship. Most individuals planning for dual-career relationships, regardless of their sexual orientation or biological sex, want partners who can be supportive of their career, can enter into an emotionally intimate relationship, and can share in the tasks of maintaining a home and family.

Table 4.3 summarizes factors identified in our research as important to young adults' decision making. As can be seen from the table, these factors range from the influence of parents' choices about occupational work and involvement in household work and parenting, to knowledge about the realities of dual-career family life, such

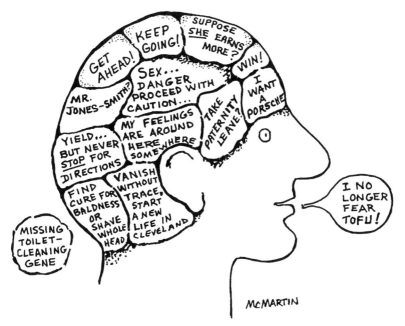

Figure 4.2. Thoughts of Average Male of Early Feminist Era, Circa 1993

as those just discussed. Some of these factors apply to lesbian and gay male dual-career relationships as well. For example, lesbian and gay male partners also are influenced by their parents' visions for their lives or how their own parents integrated work and family responsibilities.

Children learn a great deal about occupational work and family life by observing and interacting with their parents. Parents' attitudes and behaviors not only determine the family context in which children are reared but also influence children's self-concepts and visions for themselves as young adults. What parents were able to do with their talents and skills provides information to children at many levels; so does whether a father or a mother was an active participant in day-to-day parenting and household work, whether parents appeared satisfied with the choices they made, and whether parents took an active interest in their children's development, communicated certain hopes and aspirations, and/or provided

Table 4.3 Areas to Consider in Planning for a Dual-Career Relationship

---

Parents' Attitudes and Life-Style

Questions to ask yourself:

Was your mother employed? Was your father involved in household work? What did you learn from their choices about occupational work and family life? What visions does each parent hold for you as his or her daughter or son?

Young Adults' Self-Views Regarding Work and Family

Questions to ask yourself:

Do you hold the view that although both partners may be employed the woman holds primary responsibility for the home and children or do you see both partners actively integrating occupational and family roles?

How important is continuing in your own career? How important is being in a role-sharing marriage?

Essential Spouse Characteristics

Questions to ask yourself:

Do you basically view men as superior to women? Do you prefer a marriage in which the man is more capable and professionally accomplished than the woman? How important is a partner who shares in household work, who views women as equal with men, who is successful in a career, who centers his or her life around yours?

Anticipating Possible Future Difficulties

Questions to ask yourself:

How will you handle trying to locate two good positions in the same city, getting both partners to share household work, feeling competitive with a more successful spouse, deciding on child care, pushing employers to provide better family benefits and be more family sensitive?

---

experiences that broadened or narrowed their children's life views. Research indicates that parents' behaviors can strongly affect what daughters and sons see as possibilities for themselves (Hoffman, 1989). Our research, for example, indicates that young adults who perceived their parents as role-sharing are more likely to plan for role-sharing marriages than are peers reared in more traditional family environments.

Planning ahead extends to anticipating the difficulties of this emerging life-style. Other chapters of this book describe gender processes that inhibit dual-career family functioning and specific gender-related external factors that influence women's and men's choices. Anticipating the realities of a dual-career life-style makes it easier to cope with situations and difficulties when they occur.

All couples are different and need to find solutions that fit their values, personalities, passions, and needs. Couples need to consider how much each person wants to devote to her or his career at three stages: initially; when there are children, if that decision is made; and after careers are established. Some see themselves always working 50 to 60 hours a week; others prefer a solid 40 hours, and still others prefer 30 hours. During child-rearing years partners may want to consider working fewer hours. Attitudes and values about child-rearing might influence what partners look for in an employer or in a locale. Other areas crucial to the fabric of dual-career family life that need to be discussed include how partners plan to handle household work, parenting, finances, travel, and location or relocation. Planning ahead in these ways can prevent or lessen many of the struggles and concerns that generally arise. It is not always easy to make the decisions associated with dual-career relationship patterns, but planning ahead can establish goals and values that lay the foundation for the kind of relationship desired by both partners.

ȶ Summary

Increasing numbers of young adults envision possible selves in which the demands and rewards of occupational work and family are natural and not competing. Although career-oriented women more than men worry about how to integrate careers with family life, both sexes appear somewhat familiar with the realities of dual-career family life. Individuals who grew up in dual-career environments in which fathers were perceived as active participants in household work and parenting may be the most willing and able participants in dual-career family life themselves.

Jessie Bernard (1976) reminded us in the introductory quote that changing sex-specialized norms and behaviors is imperative in society today. Contemporary career-oriented young adults hold less stereotypic views of women's and men's roles, attributes, and abilities than did their earlier cohort groups, and certainly than their own parents did when they were young adults. Contributing to this change are the parents themselves, many of whom pushed for women's and men's greater equality in the workplace and in the home. I look next at the "older folks": the parents of today's young adults and the parents of children who will become young adults in the 1990s. What have their experiences been, and what can be learned from their stories?

5

❦

Living as a Dual-Career Family

Love one another but make not a bond of love:
Let it rather be a moving sea between the shores of your souls . . .
And stand together, yet not too near together:
For the pillars of the temple stand apart,
And the oak tree and the cypress grow not in each other's shadow.

(Gibran, 1923/1964, pp. 16-17)

The dual-career family represents dramatic changes in conceptions of love, enduring relationships, and social structures. Foremost among these are changes associated with assumptions of male superiority and male authority over women and of women empowering men but not themselves. Earlier chapters discuss these topics in some detail. Careers traditionally meant that those men with sufficient resources, talent, ambition, and drive moved along desired paths. Societal arrangements and custom reinforced this view. Women provided the love, nurturance, and caretaking needed to sustain men's careers—wives were the silent partners, the kingmakers, the shadows. Society, in turn, rewarded men well for their achievements while it largely ignored women's contributions to male success as well as women's capacity for independent achievement. Women were seen through men, their status and economic well-being deriving from the men in their lives. Contrary to the wisdom of the introductory quote, the pillars of the temple did not stand apart.

Unlike in earlier times, many women and men in the United States today assume that women will participate in meaningful paid work regardless of the nature of their relationships with men. More than half of women return to their jobs within one year of having a child, and 60% of employed men have employed wives. A large proportion of employed women pursue careers and these women typically become partners in dual-career relationships. In this chapter I look in some detail at these relationships and describe various aspects of family and occupational life. A more thorough treatment of this topic is available in my earlier book *Sharing It All: The Rewards and Struggles of Two-Career Families* (Gilbert, 1988).

As noted in the first chapter, the social changes necessary to view dual-career families as an egalitarian family form are slow in coming. Society remains patriarchal, although women have greater economic and legal equality with men than in the past. Men still earn much more than women on average, and men still hold most of the positions of power in the society. Moreover, individuals, regardless of their sex, still feel they must accommodate their personal lives to the traditional occupational structures if they expect to be rewarded by employers.

Challenging these snail-paced social changes are the increasing numbers of women and men who anticipate or already live a dual-career family life-style. But these women and men must still act out their private roles as spouses, parents, and homemakers within the larger world of "gendered" occupational and institutional structures and policies. Inevitable strains occur, particularly when privately decided upon principles of equality prove inconsistent with structures and policies that embody the values of male authority over women.

In this chapter I give special attention to gender processes and how they become associated not only with patterns of partners' involvement in family and occupational work but also with the inevitable realities faced by partners. Depictions of women and men in dual-career families, for example, often exaggerate stereotypic cross-gender characteristics. I recall a cover of a popular news magazine that appeared sometime in the 1980s—a harried husband and father stands over a messy stove with a toddler pulling at his apron and an infant in one arm. The accompanying cover story on dual-career families intimated that men were being made into women. Women, in turn, were shown in masculine-looking suits, carrying briefcases and being asked about "the little husband." The reality is quite different, as I shall show. Nonetheless, it is difficult to allow women and men to engage in roles traditionally assigned to the other sex and not see them as somehow "becoming" that sex. Men who devote themselves to child-rearing find their masculinity questioned. Women who aspire to "high-powered" careers are viewed as denying their femininity. The compulsion to keep certain characteristics and behaviors as female, and thus as belonging only to women, and others as male, and as belonging only to men, attests to the continuing power of conscious and unconscious gender processes in the society.

ᝄ Gender and Research on the Dual-Career Family

From a gender perspective, research on dual-career families can be viewed as falling into three distinct phases. The first phase focused on women's changing roles. Questions centered around how women could "do it all" and minimize potential harm to their traditional responsibilities of caring for husbands and children. Implicit in this approach was that women's roles were changing, but men's were not. Moreover, women were viewed as "choosing" to expand their traditional roles to include career participation, and thus as having to make whatever individual accommodations were necessary to make their "choice" possible. Close watch was kept on how women dealt with the stress of their "multiple roles," how their children fared, and how happy their husbands were.

The second phase is best characterized by the "gender as difference" perspective (see Chapter 1). Women's decisions to pursue careers were viewed as "her right" as well as "her choice." Women began to push for changes within the home and family, and hence for changes in men's behaviors. Assumptions about how to arrange occupational work and family life shifted from women themselves doing all of the accommodating to arrangements being worked out between spouses. The prevailing image of married career women changed from superwomen who did it all to egalitarian wives who shared roles with enlightened spouses. Much of the research in this phase centered on comparisons of women and men. How much were men doing in the home compared to women? Did women and men cope in different ways? Were there gender differences in marital, occupational, or parenting satisfaction?

The gender as difference phase provided important information about dissimilarities in the experiences and behaviors of female and male partners. A primary finding was that despite the talk of egalitarianism, on average wives did more of the housework and parenting, and husbands worked longer hours and earned more of the family income. Thus partners did not appear to be establishing the egalitarian relationships presumed by the Rapoports and other theorists. Attempts to understand this apparent contradiction between theory and observation moved research into its third and current phase on the construction of gender.

Recall that "it's the frames which makes some things important" (Babitz, 1979, p. 137). The gender-as-difference phase used the behavior of individual women and men as its primary focus of inquiry or "frame." Little attention was given to the larger context in which these behaviors occurred. The third and current phase, in contrast, investigates two-career family life within the context or "frame" of societal norms and practices associated with gender (see assumptions 1 and 2 in Chapter 2). Particularly important to this phase's broader perspective are the other ways in which gender becomes manifest in individuals' lives.

Current perspectives assume that how couples combine work and family depends on much more than personal wishes or preferences. For example, assumptions about how to arrange occupational work and family life, which in the second phase centered around how the two spouses could do all the accommodating between themselves, in the current and third phase centers around how workplace practices and policies can accommodate women and men who have a family life.

The next section uses current perspectives on gender to provide an understanding of key aspects of two-career family life. I explain how even behaviors that appear under partners' control, such as participating in family work and making decisions about locating and relocating, can be dramatically influenced by gender processes.

ᴥ Gender and Dual-Career Family Life

What do we know about partners who involve themselves in family life, household work, and occupations? A recent employee study at DuPont provided strong evidence that female and male employees hold increasingly similar attitudes toward relocation, business travel, and child care and that family obligations influence career planning and career experiences for women and men (Palmer, 1989). Partners, particularly the female partner, typically prefer the dual-career life-style (Ferree, 1990; Gilbert, 1988). Contrary to what was initially assumed, substantial psychological and physical health benefits occur for women and men. A number of studies document the increased benefits to partners who involve themselves in occupational work and family life (Barnett, Marshall, & Singer, 1992; Pleck, 1992; Repetti, Matthews, & Waldron, 1989). Benefits for female partners include the opportunity to develop the instrumental part of themselves and to establish a sense of self apart from a man and children, economic independence, increased self-esteem, and better overall health. For male partners benefits include the opportunity to develop the caring part of themselves and to establish a sense of self apart from being an economic provider, emotional interdependence, increased involvement as a father, and better overall health. What follows is a more detailed description of three aspects of two-career family life: (a) the spousal relationship including how partners combine family and occupational roles, (b) parenting, and (c) career advancement.

The Spousal Relationship
and How Partners Combine
Family Life and Occupational Work

> Neither of us works nearly as much as we would without kids or without each other, but I wouldn't have it any other way. (A male scientist in his thirties in a two-career science marriage, cited in Gibbons, 1992, p. 1380)

Because the dual-career family was presumed to be an egalitarian family form, researchers interpreted gender differences in involvement in household work and parenting as evidence for nonegalitarianism. Overlooked was the variability that we now know characterizes the dual-career family, and the relationship of this variability to personal, interpersonal, and contextual factors (Blair & Lichter, 1991; Coltrane & Ishii-Kuntz, 1992; Crosby, 1987; Ferree, 1990; Gilbert, 1985, 1992; Thompson & Walker, 1989). Some dual-career partners achieve a role-sharing marriage, whereas others remain fairly traditional in role behaviors within the home.

Useful to understanding this variation is Peplau's (1983) classification of marital roles into three types: traditional, modern, and egalitarian. These three types basically differ on two dimensions: power (the extent to which the husband is more dominant than the wife) and role specialization (the extent of role specialization between the spouses). According to Peplau: "Traditional marriage is based on a form of benevolent male dominance coupled with clearly specialized roles (assigned on the basis of gender). Egalitarian marriage rejects both of these ideas. Modern marriage represents a middle position" (p. 252).

Our studies of dual-career families indicate three marital types, which we labeled traditional/conventional, modern/participant, and egalitarian/role-sharing, similar to the traditional, modern, and egalitarian types identified by Peplau (Gilbert, 1985; Gilbert & Dancer, 1992). In a conventional dual-career family, both partners are involved in careers, but the responsibility for family work (household work and parenting) is retained by the woman, who adds her career role to her traditionally held family role. Typically both partners agree to the premise that work within the home is women's work, and men "help out" as long as doing so does not interfere with their career pursuits. Far more professionally ambitious than their spouses, the men in these families typically command much higher salaries and see the choice of whether to combine a career with family life as belonging to women.

In the participant/modern type, the parenting is shared by the spouses, but the woman retains responsibility for household work. In this situation, as in the modern marriage identified by Peplau (1983), male dominance is muted, and gender-based role specialization is less extensive. Most characteristic of this type is men's motivation to be active fathers, a motivation that may or may not be strongly associated with egalitarian views. They want close relations with their children but may still see other aspects of family work as the prerogative of women. Often these men wish they had closer relations with their own fathers and want to have a different kind of relationship with their own children. One man remembers feeling lost as a teenager during his father's frequent business trips: "I wanted him around but that was not an option." He made it an option for himself by selecting a company that offers paternity leave and using this option after the birth of his first child.

The third type—the role-sharing/egalitarian dual-career family—fits the description initially envisioned by the Rapoports in 1969. In this variation both partners actively involve themselves in household work and family life as well as career pursuits. This variant of the dual-career family is the most egalitarian and best represents the pattern many couples strive for. It is also the pattern that researchers initially assumed described all dual-career families. Only one third of heterosexual two-career families fit this variation, however (Crosby, 1987; Gilbert, 1985; Gilbert & Dancer, 1992; Thompson & Walker, 1989). Approximately one third of two-career families are best described by the participant/modern type and one third by the conventional/traditional type.

Marital satisfaction does not necessarily differ among the three types. Couples come to these kinds of arrangements based on a number of relevant personal and situational factors such as attitudes about family life, desired level of career involvement, and work flexibility. Table 5.1 summarizes the usual personal, relational, and environmental factors that influence how couples combine occupational and family roles. Satisfaction with the particular pattern adopted depends on these factors as well as on the degree of congruence and mutuality between partners and each partner's perceptions of fairness about the arrangements they have worked out. The last two topics are discussed at length later in this chapter.

Differences among the variations of dual-career families involve gender-related variables associated with individual partners, employment practices, and social norms. For instance, traditional male socialization equates money and resources with power. In relationships with women this becomes evident in the good provider role: Men who prove their worth by becoming financially successful are entitled to exercise control over women (Bernard, 1981). Perry-Jenkins

Table 5.1 Factors That Influence How Partners Combine Occupational and Family Roles

---

Personal Factors

- Personality (e.g., How important is a partner's need to dominate, be emotionally intimate, be number one in her or his field?)
- Attitudes and values (e.g., What are a partner's views about rearing a child, about women being as successful as men professionally?)
- Interests and abilities (e.g., How committed is a partner to occupational work, family relations? Are partners both satisfied with their occupations and career plans?)
- Stage in careers (e.g., Is one partner peaking career-wise and the other thinking about retirement?)

Relationship Factors

- Equity and power (e.g., How are decisions made? What seems fair? How do partners come to agreements about household work, parenting, money?)
- Partner support (e.g., Can partners count on each other for support in most areas?)
- Shared values and expectations (e.g., Do partners share the same views of women's and men's roles? Do they have similar life goals?)

Environmental/Societal Factors

- The work situation (e.g., Are work hours flexible? Is there evidence of sex discrimination or other kinds of gender bias? Are policies prohibiting sexual harassment in place and understood?)
- Employer's views (e.g., What kinds of family policy are provided? What is the general attitude toward employees who involve themselves in family life?)
- Child care availability and quality (e.g., Is child care available and does it met parents' criteria for quality care?)
- Support systems (e.g., Do family members lives near by? Are friends and colleagues also in dual-wage families? Is the community responsive to the needs of employed parents?)

---

and Crouter (1990), for example, found that husbands in dual-earner families who viewed men as responsible for the financial security of the family contributed less to household work than did men who saw themselves as co-providers. Similarly, husbands in traditional/ conventional dual-career families generally differ from husbands in egalitarian/role-sharing dual-career families on such indexes as dominance, needs for closeness and inclusion, and the differential between spouses' salaries (Gilbert, 1985). Men in conventional dual-career marriages typically report higher dominance needs, lower needs for closeness, and much higher salaries than their spouses. They also feel less emotionally close to spouses and to their children.

Gender processes may operate in still other ways. Interpersonal dynamics based on assumed gender-related spousal characteristics may keep husbands in the dominant position. For instance, the degree to which both partners consciously or unconsciously accept men's entitlement to female nurturance likely relates to the mutuality of spousal support achieved by couples, which in turn may influence the type of dual-career family achieved by partners (i.e., role-sharing, participant, or conventional). That is, men's expectancies that women provide support to men may be an important determinant of dynamics that develop between spouses. Although women may want the kind of support from their spouse that they themselves provide, they may not feel as entitled to ask for or receive it.

Findings from my earlier study on men in two-career families help illustrate these processes. I found that husbands' perceptions of mutuality of spousal support for partner's career differed for the three variations of families (Gilbert, 1985). Nearly all the men in conventional dual-career families (87%) said their wives were more supportive of husbands' career pursuits than husbands were of wives', and only 13% saw the support as comparable. Although participant/modern husbands (75%) were more similar to role-sharing husbands (62%) in viewing the spousal support provided by each partner as comparable, they were more like conventional husbands in that not one man saw himself as the more supportive of the two spouses. In contrast, 38% of the role-sharing men saw themselves as the more supportive spouse. Finally, unlike the other two groups of men, no role-sharing husband felt his wife was the more supportive spouse. Similar findings were reported by Ross and her colleagues (cited in Thoits, 1987).

Mutuality of spousal support and affirmation. The importance of mutual spousal support and affirmation to successful dual-career marriages cannot be overemphasized. Jessie Bernard (1974) noted some time ago that spousal support and sensitivity play a key role in dual-career families. Spousal support not only involves valuing and affirming a partner's abilities and goals, but it also involves emotional support, emphatic listening, and the ability to nurture. It requires putting aside one's own immediate needs and doing for another, as Mrs. Ramsey did for Mr. Ramsey in *To the Lighthouse* (see Chapter 2). Men typically have depended on women for support and affirmation (Pleck, 1981b). In two-career marriages, men's ability to give women the emotional support and encouragement women traditionally give to men is especially crucial to spouses' marital happiness.

Inextricably tied to the ability to be sensitive and give support is how the need for support is conceptualized by each partner and the meaning each attributes to providing support. Present views, implicitly derived from views of gender as difference, assume that the person with "needs" is lacking in some fundamental, unchanging way, and that the female partner is more needy than the male partner (i.e., the stereotypic view that women are basically dependent and stay that way and that men are rarely dependent regardless of the behaviors they may engage in). From this perspective, individuals meet one another's needs, but the process of meeting another person's needs leaves both individuals basically unchanged. Partners add up what is given to them and match this total against some internal standard or norm, such as equity, that represents what each is entitled to or should be satisfied with. An illustrative example would be a wife who relocates for a husband's position, assumes the next move is for her career, and feels resentful and underbenefitted when he balks at doing so when she wants to relocate some years later.

Partners in dual-career relationships must reframe social support as an interpersonal process involving both giving and receiving and mutual empowerment and strength, a reframing likely not necessary in lesbian couples because of the absence of gender. Stereotypically, dependency was assumed to be a personal variable, characteristic of women, not a dynamic interpersonal variable characteristic of an ongoing relationship. By reconceptualizing the relation between gender and dependency, heterosexual partners can move beyond viewing dependency as a characteristic on which wives and husbands differ to viewing dependency as an interpersonal process that serves as a vehicle for the development of mutuality between partners. To be able to rely on others and have them able to rely on you is enhancing and empowering to partners and to the relationship.

Perceptions of fairness: Equity versus equality. Pleck (1985), in his book *Working Wives/Working Husbands,* concluded that there appears to be good evidence for an inequity effect among dual-wage families. That is, from the perspective of working wives and husbands, it may not be that women are doing too much, but that men are doing too little.

The concept of equity refers to a feeling of fairness based upon an individual's perception of the overall balance of rewards and constraints in a situation (Gilbert & Rachlin, 1987; Thompson, 1991). The basis of the equity concept rests on a comparison individuals make between their own cost/benefit ratios and those of another. A central aspect of the theory on equity is the relationship between perceived equity and feelings of well-being and satisfaction; individuals in inequitable relationships are hypothesized to be dissatisfied, distressed, and motivated to restore equity or reduce inequity.

Partners are faced with working out a balance of career and family responsibilities both individually and as a couple. According to equity theory, satisfaction with a particular balance of roles is highest when each partner perceives the arrangement as fair regardless of the particular distribution of labor in the household. Spouses who perceive their relationship as equitable are expected to be more satisfied and less distressed than persons who perceive their relationships as inequitable. For example, wives who define themselves as co-providers, rather than as persons who generate a second income, feel more entitled to participation from husbands and thus feel relatively unsatisfied if they perceive their husbands as not doing their fair share of family work. Correspondingly, husbands typically involve themselves more in family work when wives make greater financial contributions to the family and when both partners attribute greater meaning and importance to the wife's employment (Barnett & Baruch, 1987b). Finally, women and men who achieve desired outcomes through family work are unlikely to be aware of injustice (Thompson, 1991). Desired outcomes might include family harmony, family time, or care and responsiveness among family members.

In a comprehensive review of the literature, Thompson and Walker (1989) saw evidence for a positive relationship between wives' marital satisfaction and personal well-being and husbands' doing their fair share of family work. Similarly, Thoits (1987) reported that the lowest stress levels occurred in marriages in which both spouses were employed, both wanted to be employed, and both shared the housework and child care. The greatest distress for both spouses was found in marriages where the wife was reluctantly employed and took full responsibility for family work.

Potential conflicts and problems emerge when a sufficient level of fairness is not achieved. In a recent study we found that although husbands and wives were in agreement that household and parenting tasks were generally distributed between the partners, they were not necessarily in agreement about how fair they thought the distribution was. Individuals in couples in which both partners saw the arrangements as fair reported higher relationship and life satisfaction than did those in which one or both partners did not. Moreover, wives more than husbands perceived a lack of fairness (Dancer & Gilbert, in press).

The apparent inconsistency between women's perceptions of equity and their reports of partner participation could reflect subtle gender processes in the marital relationship. For example, women may feel they need to "police" the agreed-upon divisions of tasks, or they may feel they still are responsible for planning and delegating, although the work itself may be quite equally shared. Either scenario may add to the woman's feelings of doing more than her fair share. Some women in two-career families also may view husbands who participate to the same extent as they do as not doing their fair share. For example, women who are more career committed or more successful than their spouses may view fairness as involving husbands doing more than the wives themselves do.

In summary, partners' assessments of fairness or equity about the balance of family and professional roles achieved by the couple are crucial to marital satisfaction and marital quality. Equality of power is not the issue, but rather the perceptions of equity or proportional returns in the exchange of personal and economic resources. Couples divide chores and responsibilities in many ways. Typically priorities are based on partners' values and interests and on the external constraints or realities of their situation. Tasks are divided in ways that seem fair (e.g., husband does tasks he likes such as cooking and laundry, and wife does those more to her liking such as paying the bills and clothes shopping). Renegotiating and flexibility are the norm in these marriages.

Parenting

> The world is full of fathers who rarely see their children [because of their careers]; for mothers [with careers] to do the same is not the answer. (Poloma, Pendleton, & Garland, 1982, p. 188)

Historically women held nearly full responsibility for the well-being of their children. Thus when both partners began to pursue careers, the big question was, "Who would mind the children?" Society took a very dim view toward employed women, particularly toward women who had preschool-aged children. Researchers initially looked for harm to children and thus focused on comparisons of children reared in traditional and dual-wage homes. Results from many, many studies showed preschool-aged children to be at no added risk if they received alternate child or day care instead of parental care for some portion of the day. This is also the case for children under the age of one (Pleck, 1992). Research interest now has moved to structural variables and hence to investigations of the kinds of care provided, definitions of optimal care, and the impact of employers' policies on family life and on spouses' well-being (Zedleck & Mosier, 1990). Chapter 6 looks in more detail at the findings of this research.

Maternal employment per se appears generally unrelated to child outcomes. Instead maternal employment operates through its effects on the family environment and the child-care arrangements, and these are moderated by parental attitudes, family structure, workplace policies, and other relevant variables (Hoffman, 1989). Obviously the more employers' policies reflect a traditional workplace culture in which women with children leave the workplace and men with children are unencumbered by family responsibilities, the more difficult it becomes for both partners to parent and for society to achieve gender equality.

As one father in his late thirties in a role-sharing marriage said: "Our son might be better off if one of us stayed home with him. But we are healthier people because we work. This will benefit him in the long run." This, then, is the crux of the kind of parent-child relationship that partners in dual-career families envision and strive for. Parenting means mothering and fathering and requires some supplemental care. Each partner develops a viable balance or integration between giving and nurturing, on the one hand, and maintaining and developing his or her own "self," on the other.

Traditionally women bonded with others, and men developed themselves. Both women and men acted on the supposition that direct caretaking by fathers was outside the male domain of competence and temperament. Women bonded with children and put aside their separate sense of self so men would be free to further develop their sense of self. The emergent view in dual-career families is that parents can respond to a child's needs and bond with their child without having to submerge their own personal identity.

As the father quoted earlier indicated, there may be additional benefits to children in role-sharing families where both parents are doing what they want to be doing and also involve themselves with their families. Studies of children reared in dual-career families indicate that respondents rated their families high in closeness. They especially noted feelings of mutual concern and support. One adolescent in our studies commented that "My parents have shown me that a female should not have to take care of the house alone and work." A number of other studies report ways children benefit when both parents are employed (Hilton & Haldeman, 1991; Hoffman, 1989; Scarr, Phillips, & McCartney, 1989). Both girls and boys, for example, develop less stereotypic gender-role attitudes, and girls gain more self-confidence and independence of spirit. Both boys and girls participate more in household work and boys in less sex-segregated household work.

Timing: Whether and when to parent? Nearly all heterosexual dual-career couples want to have a child, and the vast majority do. In fact, deciding when to have a child typically is more the question than deciding whether to have a child. Couples typically take longer than expected to "finally take the plunge," because they keep waiting for the right or best time. Most dual-career couples delay parenthood until the female partner reaches her thirties. In fact, the vast majority of women over 30 years old who give birth are in professional careers.

Women in their thirties now account for one birth in three (Wessel, 1989). Furthermore, women between the ages of 30 and 39 are far more fertile than earlier cohort groups. With the use of prenatal diagnosis and other medical procedures, the risk of an abnormal birth for women between 35 and 44 can be reduced to about the same very low level as for a woman of 34. Thus healthy women in their thirties or forties enjoy a good prospect of giving birth to a healthy infant and remaining well themselves.

The timing of the transition to parenthood has important consequences for parental behaviors, divisions of household labor, and partners' well-being (Coltrane & Ishii-Kuntz, 1992). Waiting until the female partner is in her thirties gives partners time to get established in their professions and to take on the demands of parenting at a time of greater financial stability, emotional maturity, and self-confidence. Moreover, those who wait until their thirties are more likely to define child care and housework as joint endeavors (Coltrane, 1990), particularly if both partners feel relatively secure in their occupational work and had worked out patterns of sharing housework in the years prior to having a child.

Maternal, paternal, and supplemental care. Once partners decide to parent, decisions about the child's day-to-day care are made in the context of partners' values, employers' policies, flexibility of work schedules, the availability of care, and so forth. Many couples prefer providing most of the care themselves for the first 3 to 6 months. Although employment benefits and policies increasingly recognize men as parents, it still is easier for female partners who are legal or biological mothers to ask for and receive accommodations associated with parenting.

As already mentioned (see Chapter 4), men's participation in parenting is the hallmark of the 1990s. When both parents of preschoolers are employed, studies indicate that the combined time fathers and mothers spend in direct interaction with their children is about the same as for parents in which only one spouse is employed (Jump & Haas, 1987; Scarr et al., 1989). Census data on primary child-care arrangements used by dual-wage families indicate that 14.5% of fathers provide primary care for children under 5 years of age (U.S. Bureau of the Census, 1990). Men are finding more ways to spend time at home. Increasing numbers of men use vacation and sick days to tend to children, refuse long work hours, and seek flexible schedules or family leave (U.S. Department of Labor, Women's Bureau, 1989). Pleck (1990) found that husbands in more than half the families he studied took off an average of 7.5 work days after the birth of their last child without calling it paternity leave.

Identifying quality day care is an early and important task. Many books and services are available to assist parents in locating care most consistent with partners' values and needs (e.g., U.S. Department of Labor, Women's Bureau, 1989). Most parents prefer group care for children older than three years, but they show no clear preference for individual or small-group care for children under three years. (See Chapter 6 for more detail on this topic.)

Coping with conflicts associated with parenting. Partners can experience two kinds of role conflict associated with parenting—intrarole conflict and interrole conflict. Intrarole or within role conflict has to do with meeting expectations for a particular role. A new father, for example, needs time to get comfortable with the kind of caretaking he gives to his child and may have internal dialogues with himself about what he is or is not doing. Interrole conflict, in contrast, refers to conflict between life roles. A new father also may experience conflict between his role as spouse and his role as father. His partner may want him to attend an important function for her work, and he may prefer to spend that time with his child. A more common kind of interrole conflict for parents in dual-career families occurs between their own occupational role and their parenting role. Continuing the same example, the new father may want to work half-days for several months in order to be with his child, and he also may want to head up a new project at work that requires long days for a few weeks or months.

Most people's strategies for coping with interrole conflict fall into three general types:

Understanding: Understanding the source of the stress
Management: Managing the stress
Change: Acting to change the source of the stress

Understanding strategies involve modifications in attitudes, which in turn change the meaning given to the situation causing stress. Other terms commonly applied to this type of coping include *reframing* and *cognitive restructuring*. For example, rather than berating yourself for being late to your daughter's soccer game, you feel thankful that you got there at all. A common response is to decide that for right now parenting comes first, and some things are just not going to get done. This kind of strategy is particularly effective when individuals feel assured they are doing the right thing. They feel optimistic about the long run and see everyday hassles as relatively insignificant in comparison.

Management strategies reflect attempts to "do it all." People who use management strategies try to meet all existing demands; they work more efficiently and plan their time more carefully with the idea of fitting everything in. Management-type strategies are more common in the initial stages of careers and early on in parenting. Individuals typically feel they should or must meet all the demands when they feel unsure, have less confidence, have less power and control, or are in a new situation. Because of the time and energy involved, management-type strategies are effective only for time-limited situations.

Change strategies attempt to alter or modify the situation at the root of the stress. Rather than adapting to a situation and making the best of it, or trying to do all that is asked, the individual alters behavior relevant to the situation by changing demands placed on her or him or by reducing role behaviors or roles. Examples include saying no to demands, renegotiating with a spouse or employer about certain expectations, or deciding to redefine certain life roles to allow more time for other life roles.

Most individuals use all these ways of coping at one time or another. Which strategies are used more typically depends on where one is in the career and family life cycles. Not surprisingly, the happier and more committed one is to both parenting and professional work, and the more satisfaction and happiness derived from each, the lower the conflict.

The degree of stress associated with the various kinds of role conflict varies considerably and, of course, depends on many other factors. Generally, role conflict and day-to-day stress associated with parenting and careers are lowest under the following conditions (Gilbert, 1988; Guelzow, Bird, & Koball, 1991; Kinnier, Katz, & Berry, 1991; Schnittger & Bird, 1990):

- Employers of both partners have benefit policies that are family-responsive.
- Both partners actively participate in parenting.
- Partners feel comfortable sharing the parenting with child-care personnel.
- Partners view each other's involvement in home roles as fair.
- Partners are satisfied with the child care they are using.
- Partners are happy in their occupational work.
- Partners employ understanding strategies in coping with stress.

Career Advancement

> The spouse's job, the kids—even the impact on a marriage—are factors today. (Deutsch, 1991, p. 23)

Finding a position of choice or moving from a current position may very well be the most difficult issue for members of dual-career families and one for which there is no ready or easy solution. Finding two equally attractive job offers within reasonable geographic proximity in a desired locale often proves impossible, and the more flexible partner often compromises, either by design or by necessity. Moreover, although couples often wish to give equal weight to the interests of both partners, in reality, locations or relocations among heterosexual couples often are based on the man's opportunities—either because male dominance prevailed or because various factors associated with gender made a strictly egalitarian decision impossible (Bird & Bird, 1985; Gilbert, 1985). A female spouse needing a position may be viewed by employers as less of a problem than a male spouse in the same situation because wives are assumed to more readily accommodate to husbands' occupational pursuits. Also, because women more than men desire and marry partners who are at their level educationally and at least as ambitious career-wise, placing a woman's spouse may indeed be more difficult than the other way around. Generally there are fewer higher-level positions than entry- and middle-level positions, and a woman's spouse is more likely to need a higher-level position. Finally, male applicants generally are still preferred by employers, particularly for positions above the entry level. Gender discrimination and harassment remain common experiences for women (see Chapter 2) and significantly restrict their career opportunities and salary.

The major criteria in choosing an area in which to locate or relocate are the career opportunities for both spouses and the climate or lifestyle of the area (Gilbert, 1985). Having once located in an area that partners find satisfactory, many couples, particularly those in role-sharing marriages, are reluctant to move. In fact, companies report increasing male and female employee resistance to relocating because of the reluctance of one partner to relocate if it puts the other partner at a disadvantage (Palmer, 1989). Many companies provide assistance to the accompanying spouse but even this assistance often is not sufficient to convince couples that relocating is advantageous overall to their family life (Deutsch, 1991).

Some spouses enter into long-distance commuting relations, typically for time-limited periods, or relocate for short periods of time to take advantage of a special career opportunity. These options are increasingly common for partners in the early phases of marriage who plan to enter professions that require postdoctoral training, internships, or residencies of relatively brief duration or for partners at midlife ready for a change. Other creative solutions include living half-way between two cities and adjusting work schedules to minimize commuting time.

⁂ Succeeding as a Dual-Career Family

Our evaluation of changes in the family depends on our ideas about freedom and gender, and about the possibility of gradual progress in American society. (Cancian, 1987, p. 64)

Partners in dual-career families do not and cannot exist in a vacuum. They need support in a number of areas and from a number of different sources. The various coping responses described and the resources available mediate the impact of stresses on individual partners and on the relationship. The resources helpful to dual-career families are conceptually similar to those listed in Table 5.1. There are personal, relational, and societal sources of support.

Personal resources include partners' unique characteristics such as their personality attributes, financial resources, abilities to deal with life's stresses, beliefs about love and work, coping strategies typically employed in dealing with role strain, life-cycle realities, and so forth. Particularly important to effectively managing a dual-career family are commitment to this life-style; the capacity to be flexible, compromising, and realistic; and the use of cognitive restructuring coping strategies just described (e.g., overlooking the difficulties of the dual-career life-style and focusing on the good things; seeing your family as lucky to be doing what each partner wants and managing as well as you are).

Family resources, such as spousal or partner support and sensitivity, also play a key role in dual-career families. The importance of husbands' sensitivity, which was described at length earlier in this chapter, has been noted repeatedly in studies of heterosexual couples (e.g., Barnett & Baruch, 1987a; Gilbert, 1985; Thompson & Walker, 1989; Vannoy-Hiller & Philliber, 1989). The most essential family resource is partner support, followed by support from one's own children and one's parents and friends. Shared values and expectations as well as feelings of fairness enhance the ability of spouses to be supportive. Moreover, the more supportive the spouse, the more supportive the children (Gilbert, 1988; Gilbert & Dancer, 1992).

The long-term acceptance of dual-career families requires societal resources and support (Walker, Rozee-Koker, & Wallston, 1987; Zigler & Frank, 1988). More effective coping and greater satisfaction among partners with children invariably are associated with flexibility of work schedules, family-supportive employers (and benefit policies consistent with this supportive attitude), and suitable child care (Gilbert, 1988; Guelzow, Bird, & Koball, 1991). As Chapter 6 makes clear, companies with supportive work and family policies, good health coverage, and flexible work hours have significantly less employee burnout and turnover than companies without such policies.

Areas currently receiving attention from companies fall into three categories: dependent care, including infants, adolescents, and the elderly; conditions of work such as greater flexibility in the organization, hours, and location of work; and corporate mission or the validation of family issues as an organizational concern. Currently, for example, 56% of companies offer flexible scheduling in the form of flextime, part-time employment, job-sharing, compressed work schedules, or work at home. Of the *Fortune* 500 companies, 86% have introduced new work/family programs. The reasons are many: to improve recruitment and retention, increase morale, reduce stress, and keep up with the competition (Aldous, 1990; Moskowitz & Townsend, 1991). One manager I spoke with was quick to get to the bottom line: "We're not doing flexible work scheduling to be nice. We're doing it because it makes good business sense."

ᴥ Summary

Certain realities come with dual-career family relational patterns, and partners need to be prepared for the kinds of choices associated with these realities. This chapter focused on interpersonal aspects of life in two-career marriages and thus the private lives of spouses. Theoretically, role-sharing in the private lives of heterosexual partners represents the elimination of gender-based role specialization and power associated with male dominance, as evidenced by partners' comparability and mutuality in spousal support and involvement in family responsibilities (Gilbert, 1985). I argued in the first chapter that because such marriages exist within a larger world of gender inequity, role-sharing still is best understood as an interpersonal relational characteristic rather than as a normative societal pattern. Disparate occupational demands, salary structures, employer policies, and the like can hinder or complicate one's ability to act on personal decisions of egalitarianism. Husbands continue to earn much more than wives (Brown, 1987; Hertz, 1986), and career success in organizations often requires little attention to family life (Fowlkes, 1987). There have been significant changes in employee benefits (Nieva, 1985; Walker et al., 1987), but innovations such as on-site child care, parental leave (as opposed to maternal leave), and flextime still are not generally available and are more readily available for women than men. These societal realities, conceptualized in this book as gender difference, structure, and interpersonal process, stand in sharp contrast to the assumed egalitarian nature of the dual-career family, and they impinge upon the private lives of partners and their children.

I also argued that two sources of support are crucial to the well-being of two-career families. The first is the central and extensive role of significant others, particularly the mutuality of spousal support and affirmation. The second is institutional support as reflected by workplace policies, attitudes of colleagues and employers, and the like. It is to this second source of support that I now turn.

6

❧

Workplace Family Policies

The business of America is families, and especially the children they nurture. If we skimp on their welfare, there will be no capable workers to carry on business. (Aldous, 1990, p. 365)

In earlier times questions of gender equality by and large were irrelevant in the world of occupational work. Careers were a male prerogative. Women worked in jobs and were expected to move in and out of the work force depending on the needs of their children and husbands. Also of little concern was the interplay of family life and occupational work. The worlds of family and occupations were considered separate and non-overlapping. Because family concerns had no place at work, no thought was given to the need for or importance of workplace family policies. Ideally the good provider needed to be free of family responsibilities and worries in order to better meet societal and thus employers' standards of achievement, productivity, and success.

Today both gender equality and the interrelationship of occupational work and family life are highly relevant issues for working women and men. A key question for this book is whether both can be achieved in a society in which neither have historical precedent. Are organizational structures and policies being bent and adjusted to accommodate female employees with family responsibilities, because it makes good business sense to keep them in the work force, but remaining rigid for male employees? Such a stance would perpetuate things as they are and maintain male dominance. Or are corporate changes reflecting a new organizational culture, one that recognizes the centrality of work/family policies to good business, equal opportunity, and societal well-being? Such change would increase the possibility of achieving all three factors.

In this chapter I first look at evidence for changes in attitudes and policy that have direct bearing on both the promise of gender equality and the ability to integrate occupational and family work in one's developing career. I summarize what corporations currently offer in the way of benefits, what additional benefits are likely in the near future, and what effects these benefits appear to have on employees' work performance and physical and mental health.

༄ Evidence for Changes
in Attitudes and Policies

> Work and family policies are now being viewed as a competitive tool.
> That wasn't the case five years ago. (a corporate executive officer of a
> large firm cited in Shellenbarger, 1991, p. B1)

We first look to policy makers for evidence of change—both governmental and corporate. Governmental policy can profoundly affect what employers do, and this certainly has been the case in the United States. Cases in point include child protection laws, the Pregnancy Discrimination Act of 1978, and Title VII. Title VII, it will be recalled, prohibits discrimination on the basis of sex, race, color, religion, or national origin with respect to compensation, terms, conditions, and privileges of employment and generally covers employers of 15 or more employees.

What has been the situation regarding work and family policy? Interestingly, the United States has been singularly more resistant than any other Western industrialized democracy to framing and passing legislation that would, in effect, legitimize the link between families and employment (Kamerman, 1988, 1991). Nonetheless some change is evident as the following two examples help illustrate. Both represent highly publicized bills that received a good deal of attention in the 1990s: the Act for Better Child Care and the Family and Medical Leave Act.

The Act for Better Child Care (ABC bill), drafted by a coalition that included child-care providers, women's groups, and educators, was initially introduced in 1987. It was finally enacted by Congress in late 1990, fully 3 years later, after intense and heated debate (Pleck, 1992). The act provides $27 billion over a 5-year period in the form of grants to states for expanded child-care services, tax credits to families with dependent children, and other supports for child care. The federal child-care support provided by the act is geared specifically to decreasing the number of children in inadequate arrangements. Two thirds of ABC funds will go directly to tax credits for families with children (Pleck, 1992).

The other legislation watched closely over the past few years has been the various versions of the Family and Medical Leave Act. The bill, which finally was passed by both the House and the Senate in 1990 despite the threat of a presidential veto, required companies with 50 or more employees to allow up to 12 weeks of unpaid leave to enable workers to care for newborn children or seriously ill family members. About 5% of all U.S. employers would have been covered by the bill, although they together employ about 40% of all U.S. workers. Then President Bush made good on his promise and vetoed the bill. Advocates failed to muster enough votes in the House to override the veto. No override vote was taken in the Senate. The bill was then reintroduced in the Senate in 1991, modified to some extent, and passed by the Senate in October of that year. The legislation was approved by the House in September 1992 but vetoed for a second time by President Bush shortly thereafter. Although the Senate had sufficient votes to override the president's veto, the House did not. Thus, as of November 1992, we remained without a national policy guaranteeing women or men the right to parental leave and job protection. President Clinton, however, promised to pass this bill.

Decisions at the state level have been more responsive to the family needs of employees (Wisensale & Allison, 1989). Although no state had a family leave policy in place prior to 1987, at least eight states have passed such bills to date. Three of those states, Maine, Oregon, and Rhode Island, expanded their mandates in 1991, and a number of other states have bills under consideration. None of the statutes calls for paid leave, and many restrictions apply with regard to employee eligibility (e.g., length of time with company). Generally the statutes require private-sector employers to provide medical and family leave. In Connecticut, for instance, leaves are to be phased in over a 4-year period based on size of firm and length of leave. Beginning in 1990, firms with 250 or more employees are required to grant up to 12 weeks of leave for the serious illness of the employee, to care for newborn or adopted children, or to care for seriously sick children, spouses, or parents. Beginning in July 1993, all firms with 75 or more employees will be required to provide up to 16 weeks of medical and family leave (Trzcinski & Finn-Stevenson, 1991).

Thus modest but important change has occurred under the auspices of state and federal policy. I next turn to corporate policy. Here evidence for change appears more substantial. Not only are more options available to employed parents, but also structural changes within large corporations reflect a greater commitment to work/family integration.

Structural Changes

In the past 2 years, about 300 companies have named work/family managers specifically to handle models and guidelines for different programs as well as to implement and monitor programs addressing the balancing of work and family (Bennett, 1992). Before then, although companies may have had some policies on the books, very few companies actually had a position designated for a work/family manager. Managers create models and guidelines for different programs, implement programs, and monitor their use and effectiveness. Demonstrating that programs make economic and business sense is essential to continuing a particular program. One large company is currently evaluating an emergency child-care service that provides assistance in an employee's home when a child is ill or a regular sitter calls in sick. The program is designed to save money by reducing the number of sick days that employees take.

The Conference Board, a nonprofit research group, reports that such positions have been added as companies have found policies and programs too extensive and complex to be managed piecemeal. A study by the group suggests that more companies will be adding such positions because of the growing demand for work/family programs.

A second important structural change is regular supervisory training to ensure middle management sensitivity to and knowledge of company work/family policies. Research has clearly demonstrated that work/family policies are ineffective if supervisors do not support them (Galinsky & Stein, 1990; Rodgers & Rodgers, 1989). The fact that management recognizes this barrier and is actively taking steps to educate key personnel suggests a congruence between what companies say and what they expect. Supervisors' support legitimizes the various options for employees. It is one thing to take parental leave and worry about the real consequences when you get back. It is quite another to take parental leave and know that your company supports this option because they view parenting of children as a normal circumstance of employment.

Also key to structural change are company executive officers who believe in the importance of a particular initiative. In calculating whether work/family policies make good business sense, one important factor is the bottom line: cost cutting, more competitive recruiting, lowered employee stress, and keeping the best people. Two additional important factors are vision and ideology. Companies identified as the leaders in developing work/family policies have executive officers who believe these new policies are necessary and important. For these executive officers social consciousness, perhaps informed by personal experiences, may be a justified partial explanation for corporations' family policies (see Figure 6.1, p. 108).

Changes in Work Arrangements

All the companies on the Conference Board's Work-Family Research and Advising Panel offer some form of flexible work arrangements. Over 90% of these companies offer personal leave, part-time work, flextime, and family/medical leave. Some 75% offer telecommuting, and approximately 65% offer job-sharing and compressed work weeks (Trost, 1992).

For large companies not necessarily associated with the Conference Board, the percentages are lower, as might be expected, but still impressive. A 1990 survey of 259 major employers by Hewitt Associates,

Figure 6.1. "The first item on today's agenda is to re-evaluate our traditional opposition to corporate-sponsored day care."

a benefits consulting firm, shows that 55% offer some form of child-care aid such as resource and referral services, child-care centers, or employer-assisted discounts with local child-care providers; 31% provide elder-care aid; 56% have flexible scheduling; 42% offer paid parental leave; and 14% provide adoption benefits (Trost & Hymowitz, 1990). Also, 89% of the companies surveyed offered dependent-care spending accounts, an option described later in this chapter. Finally, according to a 1991 survey by Hay/Huggins Co., a benefits consulting firm, nearly half the companies surveyed had policies providing paternity leaves, 14% offered telecommuting options, and 40% offered flexible-hours policies. In 1987 fewer of these companies offered flexible hours, and virtually none had paternity leaves or work-at-home policies. Although some employees took leave or worked at home, these situations were individually initiated and arranged (Trost, 1992).

Certain companies are considered "Stage 2" or family-friendly companies in that they offer comprehensive and multifaceted programs

responsive to employee needs (Galinsky & Stein, 1990). These companies still are greatly in the minority and receive a good deal of publicity
and recognition. At the top of the list is Johnson and Johnson, which
recently received a Department of Labor Opportunity 2000 Award
in recognition of its developing innovative employee benefit programs and its ensuring minorities and women access to higher-level
management positions (U.S. Department of Labor, Office of Information, 1991). The "Balancing Work and Family" initiatives at Johnson
and Johnson are multifaceted and include on-site child care, resources
and referral programs, family-care leave and sick days, dependent-
care accounts, flexible benefit programs, adoption benefits, relocation services, and alternative work arrangements.

IBM is another leading family-friendly corporation and was among
the first to institute flexible scheduling, leaves of absence, and work-
at-home programs. A recent leave of absence program allows employees to work part-time for up to 3 years with full company benefits.
Employees can continue the arrangement after the third year by paying part of the benefit costs. IBM also expanded its work-at-home
program, flexible work schedules, and meal-break option, which
allows employees to attend a child's school activity or meet other
family and personal needs. Other large companies listed among the
family-friendly include DuPont, Merck, AT&T (Bell Labs), NCNB,
Apple Computer, and Chevron, U.S.A. The next section of this chapter
provides descriptions of the more widely available options.

૨ What Employers Are Providing

> What is emerging is recognition that the only way companies can
> compete for the best of the new work force is by adapting to change.
> (Capek, 1991, p. 2)

A number of different kinds of programs and policies provide assistance and support to employed parents. These typically include
what are called family-oriented work policies, information services,
financial assistance, and direct child-care services. Overall more companies have policies and programs in the areas of family-oriented
work policies, information services, and financial assistance than in
the area of direct child-care services. In 1990 approximately 5,400

corporations had some kind of program to assist employees with child care, but only 30 companies had comprehensive family-friendly "Stage 2" programs (Galinsky & Stein, 1990).

Family-Oriented Work Policies

Family-oriented work policies allow parents flexibility in their work schedules and their leave time. Parents often argue and push for flexible arrangements that later become company policy. For example, a 1990 DuPont survey of their employees, 70% of whom were male, showed that 56% were interested in flexible work schedules, compared with 37% 5 years earlier. In response, DuPont has developed comprehensive, flexible work practice guidelines and is experimenting with pilot programs (Ainsworth, 1991). Policies currently receiving widespread use include the following.

Telephone access. In the past employees were discouraged from receiving or making personal calls at work. Employers now realize that telephone access to children reduces parents' stress and enhances parent-child relationships. Telephone access appears particularly important for parents with school-age children in junior high and high school who are not in after-school programs, either by choice or because such programs are not generally available.

Maternity and paternity leave. Most major companies provide for maternity disability leaves of 30 to 90 days, either paid or unpaid. A survey of 384 of the largest U.S. companies found that 95% offered disability leave for pregnancy, which included time off with some pay (U.S. Department of Labor, Women's Bureau, 1989). Fifty-two percent of the companies offered unpaid maternity leave in addition to the disability leave, and 37% offered unpaid paternity leave.

The Pregnancy Discrimination Act of 1978 ensures that pregnant women must be treated the same as other workers for the disability policy; therefore pregnant women receive the same leave time and wages as would be allowed for any other disability. Thus if a firm provides sick leave or temporary disability leave, it must allow employees to use this leave for pregnancy or childbirth-related disabilities. However, in most states employers are not required to provide a maternity disability leave for childbirth. Five states require disability insurance for all employees (California, Hawaii, New Jersey, New York, and Rhode Island), and in these states pregnant women are entitled by law to paid maternity, disability leave. Laws in 13 states require employers to hold jobs for women after childbirth, but only 2 states—California and Hawaii—provide for both job-guaranteed and paid maternity leaves.

Parental leave. Parental leave refers to time away from employment for infant care; maternity leave refers to leave for disability. Besides time off to recover from pregnancy and childbirth, parental leave provides job-guaranteed time for the care of a newborn baby, for the care of a seriously ill child, and for attention to the problems associated with the care of a seriously ill child who is under care other than home care.

At the present time, a large percentage of companies provide disability leave, but few provide separate policies for infant-care leave. A survey by the Bureau of Labor Statistics in 1989, for example, asked employees whether firms provided them leaves for a newborn separate from sick leave and vacation leave. Only 2% of the employees covered in the survey had paid maternity leave, and only 1% had paid paternity leave, that was separate from standard sick leave and vacation leave policies (cited in Trzcinski & Finn-Stevenson, 1991). Surveys in the states of Connecticut in 1990 and Minnesota in 1987 indicated that 10% to 15% of companies in these states have policies that provide for infant-care leave. Companies with 100 or more employees were more likely to provide infant care leave than were smaller companies.

Flexible scheduling. Flextime allows employees to choose arrival and departure times within a range set by the employer. Usually there is a core time that all employees need to be at work, and individuals can then schedule around that core time, for example, by coming in an hour earlier and leaving an hour earlier. Flextime helps parents match their schedules to those of their children and can also significantly reduce commuting time by allowing employees to travel at lower traffic times, and thereby maximize time at home.

Flexible work arrangements. Companies are increasingly recognizing the importance of flexibility in easing the integration of occupational and family life. Studies by the Families and Work Institute indicate that employees rank time flexibility first in their choice of what would improve their ability to balance job and family responsibilities on a day-to-day basis (Galinsky & Stein, 1990). Flexible arrangements currently available include part-time work, job-sharing, and flexplace work or telecommuting. Part-time work is not a new option and in fact was one of the few options available to employed women with young children. However, this has not been a particularly desirable option. In the past, few if any benefits were typically provided to part-time workers, and chances for advancement often were minimal. What is new is the option of part-time employment for limited periods of time or permanently with prorated benefits and little risk to career ladders. Johnson and Johnson, one of the most progressive companies with regard to family policies, instituted such a program for permanent part-time positions in 1990. Employees with a newborn or newly adopted child, ill spouse, or ailing parent may prefer part-time employment in order to spend more time with their child, spouse, or parent. By offering part-time employment, the employer is able to keep a trained and valuable employee who otherwise would have to leave the company. In addition to saving on costs of recruitment and replacement, this option builds company loyalty.

In a job-sharing arrangement two people share responsibility for a single full-time job. This can take a number of different forms. Two spouses in the same field can share the same teaching or research position, a new employee with preschool-aged children can be paired with an employee with many years of experience who wants to cut back on hours, or two employees in parallel positions can work out optimal ways to meet the responsibilities of a particular position. Finally, an option called flexplace work allows employees greater control over where they work. They may work part of the day or week at home and part at the office. Telecommuting allows employees to work from home or satellite offices, connected to the main office by computer.

Information Services

Information services are particularly popular among companies because of their low cost, high visibility, and minimal need for administrative supervision. Child-care referral agencies in most large cities offer not only child-care referral but also parent seminars and instruction on how to choose the child care that best meets parents' needs.

Resource and referral services. Under these programs a firm will contract with an outside service organization that specializes in locating child care that matches a parent's request for child care. Some agencies also may refer to home providers. The advantage of a referral service over a direct service at a company is that referral matches a parent's need for care with the type of care the parent wants and at the location the parent chooses, if the care is available. Typically firms pay the cost of the service.

Project Home Safe. Project Home Safe is a resource center for parents, child-care professionals, media representatives, researchers, and the general public. Sponsored by the American Home Economics Association and Whirlpool Foundation, its resources include tip sheets for parents on topics such as safety and after-school activities for children at home alone, fact sheets on issues involved in developing and operating supervised child-care programs for school-aged children, and a library of books and materials related to the self-care of school-aged children. Each year, five states are selected as Project Home Safe training sites. Individuals trained in those states then provide assistance to parents, educators, and community groups in their area.

Financial Assistance

Employers can provide financial assistance to help parents pay for their child-care expenses. Although financial assistance will not increase the supply of child care or help parents locate care, it may assist them in obtaining better care.

Several options are available. Some employers negotiate discounts at local child-care centers for their employees or provide subsidies for a percentage of the child-care expenses. More typically assistance is offered in the way of a tax savings through a salary reduction agreement. A large percentage of companies offer dependent-care spending accounts, a benefit option that requires little financial support from the corporation but that allows employees to put aside up to a federally set cap of $5,000 per year of their pretaxable income to defray child-care expenses. This amount typically would cover child-care expenses for a preschool-aged child. The employee saves money because no income or Social Security taxes are paid on the salary set aside for child care. The employer also saves money because it is not required to pay Social Security or unemployment taxes on salary in a dependent-care account.

Direct Child-Care Services

These kinds of services include the employers' provision of child care in child-care centers, family day-care homes, school-aged child-care programs, summer day camps, and programs for mildly ill children. An employer can sponsor a child-care center on site or near the workplace, can keep the center as part of the organization, or can hire a child-care management business or a child-care chain to operate a center for its employees.

‌‌ The Effects of Family Benefits

> If I want to take time off or see the kids in a school play or do shopping, I can do it. I'm more available and feel I am a part of the household. (a male employee at a Stage 2 company)

Research has well documented the physical and psychological health benefits to women and men who involve themselves in paid work and family life. Also well documented is the fact that work/ family conflicts can cost companies money. If no employer options are available, employees who are having problems with child care, aging parents, or other family difficulties have to live with the stress and do the best they can. Often this results in lower concentration at work, lower productivity, greater absenteeism, and poorer health.

Less well researched are the effects of work/family benefits on indexes important to employers and employees. Because family benefits are relatively recent, there has not been sufficient time to conduct extensive longitudinal studies on the effects of such benefits. Also, no clear consensus exists on what "frame" should be used in deciding what questions to ask and what would serve as valid dependent or outcome measures. If the frame is corporate benefit, indexes of success would revolve around profit and productivity. If the focus is employees' well-being, indexes of success likely still would include productivity but from the vantage point of employees' well-being rather than employers' well-being. Is a program successful if employees are happier and more productive but they choose to work less than full-time, so less total work is accomplished? Suppose programs add to dollar costs: Is the lower profit worth the increases in employee satisfaction, better parent-child relations, and more equal opportunity for women and men?

Clearly ideology plays a large part in how we frame questions about work/family policies. For example, in opposing the ABC and Family Medical and Parental Leave bills described earlier, the U.S. Chamber of Commerce argued that family responsibility is individual responsibility (Pleck, 1992). This argument rests on the premise that it is wrong to ask business to shoulder some of the costs associated with meeting family needs (Trzcinski & Finn-Stevenson, 1991). Yet, as this chapter's introductory quote, "the business of America is families," makes clear, employers benefit in the long run when children are well cared for. Should not employers then bear some responsibility for sharing the costs? When firms argue that costs would be higher if mandated leave were instituted, advocates of parental leave must rephrase the question: Are we considering the full consequences of not having a leave—the costs to children, families, societies as a whole—or are we only considering the costs to one segment? How distant a horizon are we considering: one month away, one year away, or the future well-being of ourselves as well as today's children and their children (Trzcinski & Finn-Stevenson, 1991, p. 449)?

I obviously don't have answers to these questions. What can be concluded from the available research on the impact of work/family policies is the absence of negative effects on corporate profit and employee well-being. Three studies cited by Galinsky and Stein (1990) looked at companies' perceptions of corporate child-care programs. All three studies concluded that the programs increased the company's ability to attract employees, lowered absenteeism, and improved employees' work commitment and retention. Other controlled research studies reached similar conclusions (U.S. Department of Labor, Women's Bureau, 1989). A study by the Families and Work Institute showed that allowing parental leave costs less than replacing employees permanently (Shellenbarger, 1992a). Also, when disability/maternity leave or parental leave is available, excessive leave-taking is not a problem. Less than 5% of the full-time work force were reported to be out on leave during the preceding 12 months for sickness/disability or maternity leave. Finally, evidence indicates that maternity/parental leaves not only facilitate the retention of women, but also—together with other supportive policies (e.g., flexible hours and child-care assistance)—are linked to an earlier return to work (Raabe, 1990).

On a more anecdotal note, a recent article reported benefits to General Electric Aerospace Division (Shellenbarger, 1992b). Engineering-related employees informed managers that other companies offered more progressive family-leave and flexible-hours policies and that they would consider changing jobs for better family benefits. The GE unit, which knew from past experiences that it would have difficulty recruiting new employees, responded by embracing family leave, part-time work, and flexible schedules. In the first year approximately 5% of the employees used the new options, and none left the company.

Other surveys of employees report similar attitudes. More than half of the 500 men polled in 1990 by Robert Half International, the executive recruiting firm, said they would be willing to cut their salaries as much as 25% to have more family time, and approximately 45% said they would likely turn down a promotion if it meant spending less time with their families (Ball, 1989). The DuPont survey of its 10,000 employees, already cited, showed that 40% of the respondents had considered another employer that offered more job flexibility, up from 25% 3 years earlier. DuPont also reacted by providing more comprehensive flexible benefits. This study also indicated that male employees at DuPont constitute nearly half of those who are using or planning to use child care (Palmer, 1989).

Interestingly, companies are just beginning to monitor male utilization of flexible scheduling and parental leave. This in itself appears positive in that it makes men's participation in family life more visible in the workplace and thus more acceptable to management. The data available indicate that men appear to use family-supportive policies in ways both similar to and different from women (Pleck, in press). Men use flextime to about the same degree as women but are less likely to take extended formal leaves.

⮞ Summary

Any discussion of gender equality in dual-career family life must eventually turn to organizations, the structure of occupations, and the benefits provided to employees. This chapter makes clear that both men and women are asking for more flexibility in the workplace and that many employers are responding favorably. Leading corporations and institutions have developed comprehensive work/ family policies that fit the needs of a workplace populated by women and men, nearly all of whom have family responsibilities. Eighty-six percent of the *Fortune* 500 companies interviewed by the Families and Work Institute in 1990 are introducing new work/family programs at the present time (Galinsky & Friedman, 1992).

Whether these changes represent dramatic changes in the structure and culture of organizations is uncertain. Some argue that researchers and advocates have overestimated business's response and have unrealistic hopes about the future beneficence of market forces (e.g., Kingston, 1990). What criteria corporations use to evaluate new and existing programs is unclear, and the "frames" they use greatly determine the meanings attributed to any findings.

There is some evidence, for example, that work/family benefits are more geared toward women than men and that more women than men use existing work/family options (Pleck, in press). As long as men continue to earn significantly more than women, it will make greater economic sense to families for the female partner to take leave, a reduction in hours, or part-time work in order to ease the family situation. Should this occur in most families, we would perpetuate a situation in which women bring in the second income and do most of the caretaking and men progress in careers and wield most of the power over social policy and legislation. Women's commitment to and rewards from occupational work would be limited and, in turn, so would be their leverage to challenge the gender structure of the workplace (Okin, 1989). Thus, rather than transcending traditional notions of gender and how they construct participation in family and career, we would be perpetuating these notions in slightly modified forms.

A related concern is that we may be moving from husbands making decisions about wives' daily labor to employers and policy makers making decisions about women's and men's daily labor (Brown, 1987). That is, although individual families benefit when both spouses are actively involved in occupational work and family life, the structure of occupations and other societal institutions may work against these kinds of involvements. A case in point would be the resistance of national policy makers to take actions that would better enable women and men to meet the demands of occupational work and family needs, such as the Medical and Family Leave Act.

Nonetheless much positive change has occurred. Spouses in dual-career families today are better able to live fuller lives that express the doing and caring parts of themselves. For as Bateson (1990) tells us, "we need to sustain creativity with a new and richer sense of complementarity and interdependence, and we need to draw on images of collaborative caring by both men and women" (p. 114). Women and men fortunate enough to live in these more egalitarian times are in a position to bring about the additional changes needed. The next and final chapter concerns these future events.

THREE

What's Ahead

7

❦

What Will the Future Bring for Gender Equality and Dual-Career Families?

It's really hard not to be cynical about gender equality. (comment from a young woman finishing her second year at an Ivy League university)

The future is never certain, yet we continue with our plans assuming that what we hope and work for is likely to happen. We intuitively learn to use past experiences and present insights to hedge our bets about future events. This last chapter describes my best bets for the future and what these would mean for the promise of gender equality.

As the introductory comment from a current female college student suggests, there is every reason to be distrustful and questioning about achieving gender equality in the near future. Throughout this book I have shown, on the one hand, the gap between gender equality as represented theoretically by the dual-career family form and, on the other, gendered processes and structures that reinforce both men's dominance and superiority and women's dependence on and subordination to men's needs. What will move us toward gender equality, and what can we expect in the meantime?

ва Prediction #1:
In Principle, Same-Sex Dual-Career Families
Could Benefit From Increased Gender Equity

The two-paycheck family, both in the form of dual-earner and dual-
career, is more common among lesbian couples than among heterosexual couples. (Eldridge & Gilbert, 1990, p. 44)

I began the first chapter by using bylines from *The Wall Street
Journal* to reflect changing views of work, family, and intimate relations
that appeared consistent with the notion of two-career families. In
April 1992, in this same conservative newspaper, I saw the byline,
"More employers extend benefits to gay partners." According to the
article employers increasingly are recognizing homosexual partnerships among their employees and are extending health and work/
family benefits to them.

The most obvious way increased gender equity can influence same-
sex couples is through providing needed support and resources. Yet
to reveal anything about one's personal life can put gay people at
risk with employers. The statistics for lesbian and gay dual-career
couples are not readily available, although current statistics likely
include women and men whose partners are of the same sex. Unlike
a person's race or sex, an individual's sexual orientation cannot be
determined on the basis of physical cues. The pervading heterosexual bias (Morin, 1977) that is a part of our socialization usually leads
to assumptions that everyone is heterosexual unless there is clear
evidence to the contrary. Because our society discriminates heavily
against those who are not heterosexual, gays and lesbians often collude with this heterosexual bias in order to avoid the consequences
of being identified as "deviant." In one study of working lesbians
in committed relationships, 65% of the sample indicated that they
had not disclosed their lesbianism to their employers, and 37% indicated that no one in their work environment knew they were lesbian
(Eldridge & Gilbert, 1990). A significant proportion of these women
had children.

Same-sex couples must deal with some of the same kinds of decisions and dilemmas as those discussed in earlier chapters for heterosexual couples. Many couples plan to parent. Whether, when, and how
to rear children, however, involves a somewhat different set of ques-

tions, issues, and realities for lesbian and gay partners than for heterosexual partners. Whereas heterosexual couples face societal expectations that they "should" have a child, lesbians and gay men generally are stigmatized for becoming parents (Slater & Mencher, 1991). Moreover, the "how" of having children, which typically goes unquestioned by heterosexual partners, is very complex for same-sex partners and requires resources as well as sources of support outside of the relationship. Not only are family health benefits more limited for gay and lesbian partners, but also current work/family benefit programs often assume employees are the legal or biological parents. Such assumptions make asking for and receiving accommodations associated with parenting more difficult for same-sex couples. Finally, some employees may decide against using available benefit programs for fear of making their same-sex relationship visible to colleagues.

Lesbian and gay male couples tend to derive less support from their parents and other family members and to rely more on friendship networks than do married heterosexual couples. Also, heterosexual bias and homophobia may prevent including colleagues from the workplace among friendship networks. Finding a position or moving from a current locale can be further complicated for partners in lesbian and gay couples who may be reluctant to mention their dual-career situation to employers and thus not take advantage of company-sponsored programs to assist relocating spouses.

Most women and men planning for dual-career relationships, regardless of their sexual preference or orientation, want partners who can be supportive of their career, can enter into an emotionally intimate relationship, and can willingly share in the tasks of maintaining a home and family. Early on in the book I noted that the integrating and sharing of occupational and family roles, which is "emerging" for women and men in heterosexual dual-career relations, is normative among lesbians and gay men. Lesbians, for example, grow up knowing that a man will not provide for them and hence have less conflict about whether to integrate occupational and family roles. Indeed, much of the interest and excitement about the dual-career family patterns center around changes in the power relations between contemporary women and men, changes that are crucial to viewing it as an emerging family form. The situation is obviously vastly different for dual-career relationships in which neither the power dynamics implicit in heterosexual relationships nor the norms and roles of marriage as an institution operate.

Nonetheless, the fact that heterosexual dual-career families represent an emerging family form can directly benefit women in same-sex relationships, and to a lesser extent men in same-sex relationships as well. Increased gender equity would mean higher salaries and better career opportunities for all women, regardless of their sexual orientation. Thus on this dimension both partners in lesbian couples would stand to benefit. The increased number of dual-career families also has resulted in improved work/family benefits. However, gay couples may be reluctant to use policies that would require disclosing their life style to employers. Gay men may be particularly reluctant to use policies that make obvious their involvement in family work because doing so might further exaggerate negative stereotypes about homosexual men.

In summary, greater family involvement by heterosexual men theoretically will make it easier for men in same-sex relationships to use flexible options and involve themselves in family work. Similarly, with increased gender equity, women in lesbian relationships will benefit from higher salaries and better career opportunities as well as from improved work/family policies. However, the extent to which partners can risk using work/family policies will greatly determine their increased benefit to same-sex dual-career families.

❧ Prediction #2:
Increasing Numbers of College-Educated Adults
Will Enter Into Dual-Career Marriages

> The times are changing. Change may be occurring too quickly for some, but change is not occurring quickly enough for many girls and boys limited by their gender roles to less than full lives. (Jacklin, 1989, p. 132)

Recent changes in women's and men's roles and self-perceptions have had and continue to have enormous impact in areas that range from career decisions and personal relations to societal assumptions about power and privilege. One consequence will be a continuing

Figure 7.1. "He was a mighty warrior, he built great empires, but did he have a good relationship with his kids?"

increase in the number of dual-career families broadly defined. Studies of heterosexual college-aged women and men indicate that nearly all expect to marry and to be employed, and many anticipate entering into dual-career marriages. Recent surveys show young men to be more caring and sensitive than previously and more willing to compromise with spouses on issues concerning careers and family life (McLeod, 1992). Also, men will continue to be increasingly more involved as fathers (see Figure 7.1 as an example).

However, studies also show that men plan less than women for the realities of dual-career family life, are less likely to consider career-success traits as essential in a spouse, and are more likely to assume that their future spouse will take leave or reduced hours to care for young children. Thus, not unlike the situation today, in the future women more than men will push for, and work to maintain, the dual-career family lifestyle. But unlike couples today, future couples will be better prepared for the realities of combining occupational work and family, and will have more flexible options available to them. This is particularly true of young adults who themselves grew up in dual-career and dual-earner homes.

❧ Prediction #3:
We Will See Changes in Definitions of Careers and in How Careers Are Rewarded

"Does your husband work, too?" (Cline, 1992, p. 84). Over the next 20 years a "normal career" will be replaced with many paths that people will take to be competent workers and good parents and spouses. There will be multiple starting points and paths, and multiple temporary stopping points. Two models for career paths were recently described by Strober (1990): the "sprint" model, which is the normative model today, and the "marathon" model, which may become the normative model of the future.

The contemporary "sprint" model requires intense devotion to careers in the early years of occupational work. The person has to operate at top speed because it's a short-distance race. She or he has to perform at maximum capacity in a certain number of years in order to "make it" professionally as reflected by making associate in a law firm, joining middle management, or getting promoted in academe. The career biological clock is ticking, and "if individuals reach a certain age, and don't make it, they are history." For those who make it, later years are often less productive. Many feel entitled to rest on their laurels, feel burned out, or turn their energies to something else. Another characteristic of the sprint model is that the financial reward for your long hours at the office or on the road and the single-minded devotion to work comes later—after the sprint. In fact, the promise of greater reward at some future time is a key feature of this model.

In contrast to the sprinter, the "marathoner" proposed by Strober would use a model that required steady and sustained contributions over a long period of time. Salaries would be tied to actual work involvement and contributions and would thus accelerate slowly over the years and then level out. This model would provide for a more even distribution of income over the life cycle so that employees would have more income and work fewer hours in the earlier stages of careers when they typically are also supporting and rearing young children. Dual-career couples often delay a first child until the female spouse reaches her thirties. This age represents the maximum time the biological clock can run while women try to maximize getting established in a career. Having a child earlier usually means that the woman will never get on track or back on track because she did not have sufficient time to run the short-distance race. Thus the marathon model provides greater flexibility in family planning and career development, while easing the strain of financial insecurity.

Employers currently tend to place greater value on those individuals who want to move up quickly and be "on the fast track." Interestingly we know very little about how sprinters would compare with marathoners in the long run. Are people who devote 200% of their time to occupational work for the first 10 years of their work life more productive than those who devote 100% for 20 years or more? There may be little link between long-term productivity and number of hours spent at work in the early years of a career. As career models broaden, so will the criteria for productivity and success. Today productivity means increased profit to a company or individual despite the costs to the environment, families, or personal health. Indeed, productivity often excuses malfeasance, arrogant dominance, and exploitation. Future criteria for productivity will be broader in scope and will be based on reciprocal models that take preservation of human and other natural resources into account. Among other criteria, company success will be viewed in terms of minimal negative impact on employees at all levels.

In the future, greater emphasis and reward will be given to marathon-type models. Not only are Americans living longer, but also current studies show that individuals who involve themselves in occupational work and family life are the most healthy psychologically and physically and lead more productive lives. Moreover, numerous polls show that most Americans today prefer more leisure and more time with families, even at the price of reduced material living standards (Schor, 1992). They want more from their lives than a paycheck.

✎ Prediction #4:
Women and Men Entering Dual-Career Marriages Will Be Least Prepared to Deal With the Subtleties of Male Dominance

> I do not wish them [women] to have power over men; but over themselves. (Wollstonecraft, 1792/1989, p. 71)

Early chapters describe how women traditionally give men strength but never become their rivals. Women were viewed as having power over men, to use the words of Wollstonecraft, not because women were powerful in their own right, but because men needed women to make them feel powerful—as sexual partners, as providers, and as procreators. Paradoxically, women had no power over themselves because women's raison d'être was to be selfless and devoted to others. Women were led to expect the passion of men's love to fill and gratify every need of their life.

Today women have more freedom to shape themselves and determine their own lives than have young women at any time in history. This freedom of self-definition is still very new and can be frightening —for both women and men. Women fear others' reaction to their self-definition and feel apprehensive about having the responsibility of self-definition. Men fear giving up power. Men also fear losing a crucial part of their sense of self that was based on illusory superiority to, but real dominance over, women.

The chances of achieving the promise of gender equality vary directly with the extent to which women and men insist on women having power over themselves—in marriages, the workplace, and the society at large. Holding on to and using that freedom at times is a lonely and difficult burden, particularly when tradition dampens spirits and limits opportunities. The courage and self-conviction of these women and men must be strengthened. They must understand how gender extends beyond them as individuals and operates in the structures of society as well as in the dynamics of work and family relationships. They must understand that phenomena associated with assumed male superiority and female subservience, such as sexual harassment and lower pay for women, undermine their spirits and compromise their egalitarian goals.

❧ In Closing

Gender equality would bring about a different world from the one we now know. It would be a world in which women did not look to men for security and men did not look to women to sustain their personal lives and rear their children. It would be a world without glass ceilings and glass walls. It would be a world in which women would not hear from colleagues in the halls of academia that they could not help their prejudice: "I feel bad about it, but I really do feel women are genetically inferior in math" (Selvin, 1992, p. 1382). It would be a world in which men would be as likely as women to pause in their careers for child-rearing, in which neither men nor women would be "punished" or viewed as unambitious or a "bad bet" if they identified themselves as family-oriented. It would be a world in which just as many wives as husbands earned more money than their spouses. It would be a world in which careers peaked more than once and at no set time. It would be a world in which men's time would not be too important to spend with children—their own or those of other people. And it would be a world with even greater variation in the types of dual-career families.

References

Ainsworth, S. J. (1991, August 26). Chemical firms offer employees expanded child care programs. *Chemical and Engineering News*, pp. 12-14.

Aldous, J. (1990). Specification and speculation concerning the politics of workplace family policies. *Journal of Family Issues, 2*, 355-367.

American Association of University Women (AAUW). (1991). Short-changing girls, short-changing America. Washington, DC: Author. (Available from AAUW, 1111 16th, NW, Washington, DC 20036-4873)

American Association of University Women (AAUW). (1992). How schools short-change girls. *AAUW Outlook, 86*(1), 15-25.

Archer, S. L. (1985). Career and/or family: The identity process for adolescent girls. *Youth and Society, 16*, 289-314.

Aries, E. (1987). Gender and communication. In P. Shaver & C. Hendrick (Eds.), *Review of personality and social psychology* (pp. 149-176). Newbury Park, CA: Sage.

Astrachan, A. (1986). *How men feel: Their responses to women's demands for equality and power.* New York: Anchor Press/Doubleday.

Babitz, E. (1979). *Sex and rage.* New York: Knopf.

Ball, A. L. (1989, October 23). The daddy track. *New York*, pp. 52-60.

Barbara, J., & McBrien, W. (1981). *Me again: Uncollected writings of Stevie Smith*. London: Virago Press Limited. (Original work published 1937)

Barnett, R. C., & Baruch, G. K. (1987a). Social roles, gender, and psychological distress. In R. C. Barnett, L. Biener, & G. K. Baruch (Eds.), *Gender and stress* (pp. 122-143). New York: Free Press.

Barnett, R. C., & Baruch, G. K. (1987b). Determinants of fathers' participation in family work. *Journal of Marriage and the Family, 49,* 29-40.

Barnett, R. C., Marshall, N. L., & Singer, J. D. (1992). Job experiences over time, multiple roles, and women's mental health: A longitudinal study. *Journal of Personality and Social Psychology, 62,* 634-644.

Barringa, M. (1991). Sexism charged by Stanford physician. *Science, 252,* 1484.

Bateson, M. C. (1990). *Composing a life.* New York: Penguin.

Belkin, L. (1989, August 20). Bars to equality of sexes seen as eroding slowly. *The New York Times,* pp. 1, 26.

Bennett, A. (1992, April 14). Work-family programs get their own managers. *The Wall Street Journal,* p. B1.

Bernard, J. (1974). *The future of motherhood.* New York: Dial.

Bernard, J. (1976). Change and stability in sex-role norms and behaviors. *Journal of Social Issues, 32,* 207-223.

Bernard, J. (1981). The good provider role: Its rise and fall. *American Psychologist, 36,* 1-12.

Bernard, J. (1982). *The future of marriage.* New Haven, CT: Yale University Press.

Betz, N. E., & Fitzgerald, L. F. (1987). *The career psychology of women.* Orlando, FL: Academic Press.

Bird, G. A., & Bird, G. W. (1985). Determinants of mobility in two-earner families: Does the wife's income count? *Journal of Marriage and the Family, 47,* 753-758.

Blair, S. L., & Lichter, D. T. (1991). Measuring the division of household labor. *Journal of Family Issues, 12,* 91-113.

Block, J. H. (1984). *Sex role identity and ego development.* San Francisco: Jossey-Bass.

Bly, R. (1991). *Iron John.* New York: Addison-Wesley.

Brannon, R. (1985). A scale for measuring attitudes about masculinity. In A. Sargent (Ed.), *Beyond sex roles* (pp. 110-116). St. Paul, MN: West Publishing.

Brehm, S. S. (1988). *Seeing female: Social roles and personal lives.* New York: Greenwood.

Brod, H. (Ed.). (1987). *The making of masculinities—The new men's studies.* Boston: Allen & Unwin.

Brown, C. A. (1987). The new patriarchy. In C. Bose, R. Feldberg, & N. Sokoloff (Eds.), *Hidden aspects of women's work* (pp. 137-160). New York: Praeger.

Brush, S. G. (1991). Women in science and engineering. *American Scientist, 79,* 404-419.

Cancian, F. M. (1987). *Love in America: Gender and self-development.* New York: Cambridge University Press.

Capek, M. E. S. (1991, April). *Summary of beyond parent tracks: Alliances for the '90s.* (Available from the National Council for Research on Women, 47-49 East 65th St., New York, NY 10021).

Catalyst. (1987). *New roles for women and men: A report on an educational intervention with college students.* (Available from 250 Park Ave. South, New York, NY 10003).

Chassler, S. (1984, August). Listening. *Ms.*, pp. 51-53, 98-100.

Clatterbaugh, K. (1990). *Contemporary perspectives on masculinity: Men, women, and politics in modern society.* Boulder, CO: Westview Press.

Cline, R. (1985, December 23). Cartoon caption. *The New Yorker*, p. 38.

Cline, R. (1992, February 24). Cartoon caption. *The New Yorker*, p. 84.

Cole, J. R. (1981). Women in science. *American Scientist, 69*, 385-391.

Coltrane, S. (1990). Birth timing and the division of labor in dual earner families: Exploratory findings and suggestions for future research. *Journal of Family Issues, 11*, 157-181.

Coltrane, S., & Ishii-Kuntz, M. (1992). Men's housework: A life course perspective. *Journal of Marriage and the Family, 54*, 43-57.

Covin, T. J., & Brush, C. C. (1991). An examination of male and female attitudes toward career and family issues. *Sex Roles, 25*, 393-415.

Crosby, F. J. (Ed.). (1987). *Spouse, parent, worker: On gender and multiple roles.* New Haven, CT: Yale University Press.

Crouter, A. C., Perry-Jenkins, M., Huston, T. L., & McHale, S. M. (1987). Processes underlying father involvement in dual-earner and single-earner families. *Developmental Psychology, 23*, 431-440.

Dancer, L. S., & Gilbert, L. A. (in press). Spouses' family work participation and its relation to wives' occupational level. *Sex Roles.*

Davis, B. M., & Gilbert, L. A. (1989). Effect of dispositional and situational influences on women's dominance expression in mixed-sex dyads. *Journal of Personality and Social Psychology, 57*, 294-300.

Deaux, K. (1984). From individual differences to social categories: Analysis of a decade's research on gender. *American Psychologist, 39*, 105-116.

Deaux, K. (1985). Sex and gender. *Annual Review of Psychology, 36*, 49-81.

de Beauvoir, S. (1970). *The second sex.* New York: Bantam.

Deutsch, C. H. (1991, May 12). Computing the assignment abroad. *The New York Times*, p. F23.

Doyle, J. A. (1989). *The male experience* (2nd ed.). Dubuque, IA: William C. Brown.

Eagly, A. H. (1991, August). *Gender and leadership.* Invited address at the Annual Meeting of the American Psychological Association, San Francisco, CA.

Eccles, J. S. (1987). Gender roles and women's achievement-related decisions. *Psychology of Women Quarterly, 11*, 135-172.

Eccles, J. S., Jacobs, J. E., & Harold, R. D. (1990). Gender role stereotypes, expectancy effects, and parents' socialization of gender differences. *Journey of Social Issues, 46*(2), 183-201.

Eldridge, N. S., & Gilbert, L. A. (1990). Correlates of relationship satisfaction in lesbian couples. *Psychology of Women Quarterly, 14,* 43-62.

Erikson, E. (1968). *Identity, youth, and crisis.* New York: Norton.

Faludi, S. (1991). *Backlash: The undeclared war against American women.* New York: Crown.

Farmer, H. S. (1985). Model of career and achievement motivation for women and men. *Journal of Counseling Psychology, 32,* 363-390.

Fausto-Sterling, A. (1985). *Myths of gender: Biological theories about women and men.* New York: Basic Books.

Feingold, A. (1988). Cognitive gender differences are disappearing. *American Psychologist, 43,* 95-103.

Ferree, M. M. (1990). Beyond separate spheres: Feminism and family research. *Journal of Marriage and the Family, 52,* 866-884.

Flexner, E. (1959). *Century of struggle: The women's rights movement in the United States.* Cambridge, MA: Harvard University Press.

Fowlkes, M. R. (1980). *Behind every successful man: Wives of medicine and academe.* New York: Columbia University Press.

Fowlkes, M. R. (1987). The myth of merit and male professional careers: The roles of wives. In N. Gerstel & H. E. Gross (Eds.), *Families and work* (pp. 347-360). Philadelphia: Temple University Press.

Freud, S. (1933). *New introductory lectures.* New York: Norton.

Fuchsberg, G. (1992, February 24). Change is slow in views on two-career couples. *The Wall Street Journal,* p. B1.

Galinsky, E., & Friedman, D. E. (1992). *Corporate reference guide to work-family programs.* New York: Families and Work Institute.

Galinsky, E., & Stein, P. J. (1990). The impact of human resource policies on employees: Balancing work/family life. *Journal of Family Issues, 11,* 368-383.

Ganong, L. H., & Coleman, M. (1992). Gender differences in expectations of self and future partner. *Journal of Family Issues, 13,* 55-64.

Gates, A. (1989). *Fringe benefits.* New York: Dell.

Gibbons, A. (1992, March 13). Key issue: Two-career science marriage. *Science, 255,* 1380-1382.

Gibran, K. (1964). *The prophet.* New York: Knopf. (Original work published 1923)

Gilbert, L. A. (1985). *Men in dual-career families: Current realities and future prospects.* Hillsdale, NJ: Lawrence Erlbaum.

Gilbert, L. A. (Ed.). (1987a). Dual-career families in perspective. *The Counseling Psychologist, 15*(1).

Gilbert, L. A. (1987b). Female and male emotional dependency and its implications for the therapist-client relationship. *Professional Psychology: Research and Practice, 18,* 555-561.

Gilbert, L. A. (1988). *Sharing it all: The rewards and struggles of two-career families.* New York: Plenum.

Gilbert, L. A. (1992). Gender and counseling psychology: Current knowledge and directions for research and social action. In S. D. Brown & R. W. Lent (Eds.), *Handbook of counseling psychology* (pp. 383-416). New York: John Wiley.

Gilbert, L. A., & Dancer, L. S. (1992). Dual-earner families in the United States and adolescent development. In S. Lewis, D. N. Izraeli, & H. Hootsmans (Eds.), *Dual-earner families: International perspectives* (pp. 151-171). Newbury Park, CA: Sage.

Gilbert, L. A., Dancer, L. S., Rossman, K. M., & Thorn, B. L. (1991). Assessing perceptions of occupational-family integration. *Sex Roles, 24,* 107-119.

Gilbert, L. A., & Rachlin, V. (1987). Mental health and psychological functioning of dual-career families. *The Counseling Psychologist, 15,* 7-49.

Gilbert, L. A., & Rossman, K. M. (1992). Gender and the mentoring process for women: Implications for professional development. *Professional Psychology: Research and Practice, 23,* 233-238.

Gilbert, L. A., Rossman, K. M., Hallett, M. B., & Habib, K. (1992, July). *Father's involvement in family work and its relation to adolescents' gender-related self-concepts.* Paper presented at the meetings of the 25th International Congress of Psychology, Brussels.

Gilbert, L. A., Rossman, K. M., & Thorn, B. L. (1991, June). *Perceptions of occupational-family integration in young adults: The influence of parents' choices.* Paper presented at the meeting of the American Psychological Society, Dallas, TX.

Gill, B. (1990, April 2). The sky line: Homage to Mumford. *The New Yorker,* pp. 90-93.

Gilman, C. P. (1914). *The man-made world or our androcentric culture.* New York: Charlton.

Gilmore, D. D. (1990). *Manhood in the making: Cultural concepts of masculinity.* New Haven, CT: Yale University Press.

Goldberg, H. (1976). *The hazards of being male: Surviving the myth of masculine privilege.* New York: Signet.

Goode, W. J. (1982). Why men resist. In B. Thorne (Ed.), *Rethinking the family: Some feminist questions* (pp. 131-150). White Plains, NY: Longman.

Guelzow, M. G., Bird, G. W., & Koball, E. H. (1991). An exploratory path analysis of the stress process for dual-career men and women. *Journal of Marriage and the Family, 53,* 151-164.

Guisewite, C. (1988, January 26). Cathy. *Austin American-Statesman,* Sunday comics.

Gutek, B. A. (1986). *Sex and the workplace.* San Francisco: Jossey-Bass.

Gutek, B. A. (1989, March). *Sexual harassment: A source of stress for employed women.* Paper presented at the Radcliffe Conference on Women in the 21st Century, Cambridge, MA.

Hamilton, W. (1983, June 13). Cartoon caption. *The New Yorker,* p. 62.

Hamilton, W. (1987, December 7). Cartoon caption. *The New Yorker,* p. 140.

Hare-Mustin, R. T. (1991). Sex, lies, and headaches: The problem is power. *Journal of Feminist Family Therapy, 3*(1/2), 39-61.

Hare-Mustin, R. T., & Marecek, J. (1990). *Making a difference: Psychology and the construction of gender.* New Haven, CT: Yale University Press.

Heilbrun, C. G. (1988). *Writing a woman's life.* New York: Ballantine.

Hertz, R. (1986). *More equal than others: Men and women in dual-career marriages.* Berkeley: University of California Press.

Hilton, J. M., & Haldeman, V. A. (1991). Gender differences in the performance of household tasks by adults and children in single-parent and two-parent, two-earner families. *Journal of Family Issues, 12,* 114-130.

Hodnett, J. (1991). *Correlates of relationship satisfaction among dual-career gay male couples.* Unpublished doctoral dissertation, University of Texas at Austin.

Hoffman, L. W. (1989). Effects of maternal employment in the two-parent family. *American Psychologist, 44,* 283-292.

Holland, D. C., & Eisenhart, M. A. (1990). *Educated in romance: Women, achievement, and college culture.* Chicago: University of Chicago Press.

Horrigan, M. W., & Markey, J. P. (1990, July). Recent gains in women's earnings: Better pay or longer hours. *Monthly Labor Review,* 11-17.

Hyde, J. S. (1991, August). *Gender and sex: So what has meta-analysis done for me?* G. Stanley Hall Lecture presented at the annual meeting of the American Psychological Association, San Francisco, CA.

Hyde, J. S., & Clark, R. (1988, August). *Maternity leave: The mother's perspective.* Paper presented at the annual meeting of the American Psychological Association, Atlanta, GA.

Hyde, J. S., & Essex, M. J. (Eds.). (1991). *Parental leave and child care: Setting a research and policy agenda.* Philadelphia: Temple University Press.

Ibsen, H. (1959). A doll's house. In R. F. Sharp (Trans.), *Four great plays by Henrik Ibsen* (pp. 1-68). New York: Bantam. (Original work published 1879)

Jacklin, C. N. (1989). Female and male: Issues of gender. *American Psychologist, 44,* 127-133.

Jump, T. L., & Haas, L. (1987). Fathers in transition: Dual-career fathers' participation in child care. In M. S. Kimmel (Ed.), *Changing men: New directions in research on men and masculinity* (pp. 98-114). Newbury Park, CA: Sage.

Kahn, A. S. (1984). The power war: Male responses to power loss under equality. *Psychology of Women Quarterly, 8,* 234-247.

Kamerman, S. B. (1988). Maternity and parenting benefits: An international overview. In E. F. Zigler & M. Frank (Eds.), *The parental leave crisis: Toward a national policy* (pp. 235-244). New Haven, CT: Yale University Press.

Kamerman, S. B. (1991). Child care policies and programs: An international overview. *Journal of Social Issues, 47*(2), 179-196.

Keller, E. F., & Moglen, H. (1987). Competition and feminism: Conflicts for academic women. *Signs, 12*(3), 493-511.

Keller, E. F. (1985). *Reflections on gender and science*. New Haven, CT: Yale University Press.

Kelley, S. (1991, July 7). Cartoon caption. *The New York Times*, p. 2E.

Kimmel, M. S. (1989). From pedestals to partners: Men's responses to feminism. In J. Freeman (Ed.), *Women: A feminist perspective* (4th ed., pp. 581-594). Mountain View, CA: Mayfield.

Kimmel, M. S., & Messner, M. A. (Eds.). (1989). *Men's lives*. New York: Macmillan.

Kingston, P. W. (1990). Illusions and ignorance about the family-responsive workplace. *Journal of Family Issues, 11*, 438-454.

Kinnier, R. T., Katz, E. C., & Berry, M. A. (1991). Successful resolutions to the career-versus-family conflict. *Journal of Counseling and Development, 69*, 439-444.

Koren, E. (1979, December 10). Cartoon caption. *The New Yorker*, p. 116.

Koss, M. P. (1990). The women's mental health research agency: Violence against women. *American Psychologist, 45*, 374-380.

Kram, K. E. (1988). *Mentoring at work: Developmental relationships in organizational life*. New York: University Press of America.

Le Guin, U. K. (1991, June 2). Breakout from the doll's house. [Review of *Alva Myrdal: A daughter's memoir*]. *The New York Times Book Review*, p. 13.

Lerner, H. E. (1983). Female dependency in context: Some theoretical and technical considerations. *American Journal of Orthopsychiatry, 53*, 697-705.

Lublin, J. S. (1991, December 30). Rights law to spur shifts in promotions. *The Wall Street Journal*, pp. B1, B4.

MacKinnon, C. (1979). *Sexual harrassment of working women*. New Haven, CT: Yale University Press.

Malcolm, A. H. (1991, June 16). A day of celebration for a more active kind of dad. *The New York Times*, p. 14.

Margolies, L., Becker, M., & Jackson-Brewer, K. (1987). Internalized homophobia: Identifying and treating the oppressor within. In Boston Lesbian Psychologies collective (Eds.), *Lesbian psychologies: Explorations and challenges* (pp. 229-241). Urbana: University of Illinois Press.

Markus, H., & Nurius, P. (1986). Possible selves. *American Psychologist, 41*, 954-969.

McGill, M. E. (1985). *The McGill report on male intimacy*. New York: Holt, Rinehart, & Winston.

McLeod, R. G. (1992, March 14). Poll on male attitudes finds '90s men sensitive, caring. *Austin American-Statesman*, pp. A1, A15.

Mill, J. S. (1970). *The subjection of women*. Cambridge: MIT Press. (Original work published 1869)

Miller, J. (1991). *Seductions: Studies in reading and culture*. London: Virago.

Morin, S. F. (1977). Heterosexual bias in psychological research on lesbianism and male homosexuality. *American Psychologist, 32*, 629-637.

Morrison, A. M., & Glinow, M. V. (1990). Women and minorities in management. *American Psychologist, 45,* 200-208.

Morrison, A. M., White, R. P., Velsor, E. V., & The Center for Creative Leadership (1987). *Breaking the glass ceiling: Can women reach the top of America's largest corporations?* New York: Addison-Wesley.

Moskowitz, M., & Townsend, C. (1991, October). The 85 best companies for working mothers. *Working Mother,* pp. 29-70.

National Science Foundation. (1991). *Selected data on science and engineering doctorate awards.* Washington, DC: Author.

Nieva, V. F. (1985). Work and family linkages. In L. Larwood, A. Stromberg, & B. A. Gutek (Eds.), *Women and work* (pp. 165-190). Beverly Hills, CA: Sage.

Okin, S. M. (1989). *Justice, gender, and the family.* New York: Basic Books.

O'Neil, J. M. (1982). Gender-role conflict and strain in men's lives. In K. Soloman & N. B. Levy (Eds.), *Men in transition* (pp. 5-44). New York: Plenum.

O'Neil, J. M. (in press). Men's and women's gender role journeys: Metaphors for healing, transition, and transformation. In B. Wainrib (Ed.), *Gender issues across the life cycle.* New York: Springer.

Palmer, G. (1989, January 5). Report of the DuPont work and family committee. *Dupont Corporate News.*

Peplau, L. A. (1983). Roles and gender. In H. H. Kelley, E. Berscheid, A. Christensen, J. H. Harvey, T. L. Huston, G. Levinger, E. McClintock, L. A. Peplau, & D. R. Peterson (Eds.), *Close relationships* (pp. 220-264). New York: Freeman.

Perry-Jenkins, M., & Crouter, A. C. (1990). Men's provider role attitudes: Implications for household work and marital satisfaction. *Journal of Family Issues, 11,* 136-156.

Pharr, S. (1988). *Homophobia: A weapon of sexism.* Little Rock, AR: Chardon.

Pleck, J. H. (1981a). *The myth of masculinity.* Cambridge: MIT Press.

Pleck, J. H. (1981b). Men's power with women, other men, and society: A men's movement analysis. In R. A. Lewis (Ed.), *Men in difficult times: Masculinity today and tomorrow* (pp. 234-244). New York: Prentice-Hall.

Pleck, J. H. (1985). *Working wives/working husbands.* Beverly Hills, CA: Sage.

Pleck, J. H. (1987). American fathering in historical perspective. In M. S. Kimmel (Ed.), *Changing men: New directions in research on men and masculinity* (pp. 83-97). Newbury Park, CA: Sage.

Pleck, J. H. (1990, August). *Family-supportive employer policies and men's participation.* Paper presented at the annual meeting of the American Psychological Association, Boston, MA.

Pleck, J. H. (1992). Work-family policies in the United States. In H. Kahne & J. Giele (Eds.), *Women's lives and women's work: Parallels and contrasts in modernizing and industrial countries.* Boulder, CO: Westview.

Pleck, J. H. (in press). Are "family-supportive" employer policies relevant to men? In J. C. Hood (Ed.), *Work, family, and masculinities*. Newbury Park, CA: Sage.

Pogrebin, L. C. (1983). *Family politics: Love and power on an intimate frontier.* New York: McGraw-Hill.

Poloma, M. M., Pendleton, B. F., & Garland, T. N. (1982). Reconsidering the dual-career marriage: A longitudinal approach. In J. Aldous (Ed.), *Two paychecks: Life in dual-earner families* (pp. 173-192). Beverly Hills, CA: Sage.

Prose, F. (1990, January 7). Confident at 11, confused at 16. *The New York Times Magazine*, pp. 22-25, 37-40, 45-46.

Raabe, P. H. (1990). The organizational effects of workplace family policies: Past weaknesses and recent progress. *Journal of Family Issues, 11*, 477-491.

Rapoport, R., & Rapoport, R. N. (1969). The dual-career family. *Human Relations, 22*, 3-30.

Repetti, R. L., Matthews, K. A., & Waldron, I. (1989). Employment and women's health: Effects of paid employment on women's mental and physical health. *American Psychologist, 44*, 1394-1401.

Rich, A. (1979). *On lies, secrets, and silence.* New York: Norton.

Richards, D. (1991, February 17). The last of the red hot playwrights. *The New York Times Magazine*, pp. 30-32, 36, 64.

Rix, S. E. (Ed.). (1987). *The American woman 1987-88: A report in depth.* New York: Norton.

Rodgers, F. S., & Rodgers, C. (1989). Business and the facts of family life. *Harvard Business Review, 89*, 121-129.

Rose, S., & Larwood, L. (1988). *Women's careers: Pathways and pitfalls.* New York: Praeger.

Scarr, S., Phillips, D., & McCartney, K. (1989). Working mothers and their families. *American Psychologist, 44*, 1402-1409.

Schneider, M. S. (1986). The relationships of cohabiting lesbian and heterosexual couples: A comparison. *Psychology of Women Quarterly, 10*, 234-239.

Schnittger, M. H., & Bird, G. W. (1990). Coping among dual-career men and women across the family life cycle. *Family Relations, 39*, 199-205.

Schor, J. B. (1992). *The overworked American: The unexpected decline of leisure.* New York: Basic Books.

Schwartz, F. N. (1989, January/February). Management women and the new facts of life. *Harvard Business Review, 1*, 65-76.

Scott, J. W. (1982). The mechanization of women's work. *Scientific American, 247*, 167-185.

Selvin, P. (1992, March 13). Profile of a field: Mathematics. *Science, 255*, 1382-1385.

Shellenbarger, S. (1991, November 15). More job seekers put family needs first. *The Wall Street Journal*, pp. B1, B4.

Shellenbarger, S. (1992a, February 12). GE unit sees advantage in more family benefits. *The Wall Street Journal*, p. B1.

Shellenbarger, S. (1992b, April 3). Employers try to see if family benefits pay. *The Wall Street Journal*, p. B1.

Shelley, P. B. (1965). *Prometheus unbound*. The Netherlands: Joh. Enschedé en zonen. (Original work published 1829)

Sherif, C. (1982). Needed concepts in the study of gender identity. *Psychology of Women Quarterly, 6*, 375-398.

Simmons, T. (1988, November 4). A mother's son. *The New York Times Magazine*, p. 9.

Sky-Peck, K. (1991). *A mother's journal*. Boston: Little, Brown.

Slater, S., & Mencher, J. (1991). The lesbian family lifecycle: A contextual approach. *American Journal of Orthopsychiatry, 6*, 372-382.

Spade, J. Z., & Reese, C. A. (1991). We've come a long way, maybe: College students' plans for work and family. *Sex Roles, 24*, 309-322.

Spain, D. (1988, November). *Women's demographic past, present, and future*. Paper presented at the Radcliffe Conference on Women in the 21st Century, Cambridge, MA.

Strober, M. (1990, November 16). *Needed research to address work/family issues*. Paper presented at Beyond Parent Tracks: Alliances for the '90s, San Francisco, CA. (Available from the National Council for Research on Women, 47-49 East 65th St., New York, NY 10021)

Tannen, D. (1990). *You just don't understand: Women and men in conversation*. New York: William Morrow.

Thoits, P. A. (1987). Negotiating roles. In F. J. Crosby (Ed.), *Spouse, parent, worker: On gender and multiple roles* (pp. 11-22). New Haven, CT: Yale University Press.

Thompson, L. (1991). Family work: Women's sense of fairness. *Journal of Family Issues, 12*, 181-196.

Thompson, L., & Walker, A. J. (1989). Women and men in marriage, work, and parenthood. *Journal of Marriage and the Family, 51*, 845-872.

Tidball, M. E. (1989). Women's colleges: Exceptional conditions, not exceptional talent, produce high achievers. In C. S. Pearson (Ed.), *Educating the majority* (pp. 157-172). Washington, DC: American Council on Education.

Tittle, C. K. (1981). *Careers and family: Sex roles and adolescent life plans*. Beverly Hills, CA: Sage.

Trost, C. (1992, February 18). To cut costs and keep the best people, more concerns offer flexible work plans. *The Wall Street Journal*, pp. B1, B7.

Trost, C., & Hymowitz, C. (1990, June 18). Careers start giving in to family needs. *The Wall Street Journal*, pp. B1, B5.

Trzcinski, E., & Finn-Stevenson, M. (1991). A response to arguments against mandated parental leave: Findings from the Connecticut survey of parental leave policies. *Journal of Marriage and the Family, 53*, 445-460.

Unger, R. K. (1990). Imperfect reflections of reality. In R. T. Hare-Mustin & J. Marecek (Eds.), *Making a difference: Psychology and the construction of gender*. New Haven, CT: Yale University Press.

U.S. Bureau of Labor Statistics. (1989). *Labor force statistics derived from the current population survey: A databook.* Washington, DC: Government Printing Office.

U.S. Bureau of Labor Statistics. (1991). *Labor force statistics derived from the current population survey: A databook.* Washington, DC: Government Printing Office.

U.S. Bureau of the Census. (1990, July). *Who's minding the kids?* (Series P-70, no. 20). Washington, DC: Government Printing Office.

U.S. Department of Education. (1988). *Report from the Office of Educational Research and Improvement.* Washington, DC: Government Printing Office.

U.S. Department of Education. (1991). *Women at thirtysomething: Paradoxes of attainment.* Washington, DC: Government Printing Office.

U.S. Department of Labor. (1991). *A report on the glass ceiling initiative.* Washington, DC: Government Printing Office.

U.S. Department of Labor, Office of Information. (1991, September 19). Secretary Martin honors contractors for outstanding programs to encourage a diverse workplace and to break the glass ceiling. *U.S. Department of Labor News,* pp. 1-5.

U.S. Department of Labor, Women's Bureau. (1989). *Employers and child care: Benefiting work and family.* Washington, DC: Government Printing Office.

U.S. Department of Labor, Women's Bureau. (1990a, September). *20 facts on women workers.* Washington, DC: Government Printing Office.

U.S. Department of Labor, Women's Bureau. (1990b, October). *Earnings differences between women and men.* Washington, DC: Government Printing Office.

U.S. Department of Labor, Women's Bureau. (1991). *Facts on working women.* Washington, DC: Government Printing Office.

Vannoy-Hiller, D., & Philliber, W. W. (1989). *Equal partners: Successful women in marriage.* Newbury Park, CA: Sage.

Verba, S. (1983). *Unwanted attention: Report on a sexual harrassment survey.* Report to the Faculty of Arts and Sciences, Harvard University. (Available from Office of the Dean, Cambridge, MA 02138)

Walker, L. S., Rozee-Koker, P., & Wallston, B. S. (1987). Social policy and the dual-career family: Bringing the social context into counseling. *The Counseling Psychologist, 15,* 97-121.

Weiss, R. (1987, September 19). Significant other. *The New York Times Magazine,* p. 10.

Weiss, R. S. (1991). *Staying the course: The emotional and social lives of men who do well at work.* New York: Free Press.

Wessel, D. (1989, June 22). Census Bureau study finds shift in fertility patterns. *The Wall Street Journal,* p. B1.

Westkott, M. (1986). *The feminist legacy of Karen Horney.* New Haven, CT: Yale University Press.

Whiting, B. B., & Edwards, C. P. (1988). *Children of different worlds: The formation of social behavior.* Cambridge, MA: Harvard University Press.

Wisensale, S. K., & Allison, M. D. (1989). Family leave legislation: State and federal initiatives. *Family Relations, 38,* 182-189.

Wollstonecraft, M. (1989). *A vindication of the rights of women.* Buffalo, NY: Prometheus Books. (Original work published 1792)

Woolf, V. (1955). *To the lighthouse.* New York: Harcourt, Brace & World. (Original work published 1927)

Woolf, V. (1957). *A room of one's own.* New York: Harcourt, Brace & Jovanovich. (Original work published 1929)

Zedleck, S., & Mosier, K. L. (1990). Work in the family and employing organization. *American Psychologist, 45,* 240-251.

Zigler, E. F., & Frank, M. (Eds.). (1988). *The parental leave crisis: Toward a national policy.* New Haven, CT: Yale University Press.

Name Index

Subject Index

❦

About the Author

Lucia Albino Gilbert is Professor of Educational Psychology at The University of Texas at Austin and teaches in the department's doctoral program in counseling psychology. She has published numerous books, chapters, and articles in the areas of gender roles and mental health, dual-career families, and the career development of women. Her first book, *Men in Dual-Career Families: Current Realities and Future Prospects,* was published in 1985 and her second book, *Sharing It All: The Rewards and Struggles of Dual-Career Families,* in 1988. An associate editor of *Psychology of Women Quarterly,* she currently serves on the editorial boards of the *Journal of Family Issues* and *Contemporary Psychology.* She has received two teaching excellence awards during her 15 years at the University of Texas at Austin and is also the recipient of the John Holland Award for Excellence in Research. She is very committed to the educational process and often speaks to representatives from the media (radio, television, magazines) as well as to professional and lay audiences on topics associated with her major areas of research and teaching.